Manual 3

YOUNG WOMEN
Fun-tastic! Activities

You'll find activities to match Lessons #1-47:

❀ Young Woman's Value-able Journal
❀ Lesson Activities to Place in Journal
❀ Midweek Activities
❀ Thought Treats
❀ Scripture Cards

❀ *"Bloom Where You're Planted"*
7 Floral Symbols to Color-Code Value Journal

GOSPEL BASIC SUBJECTS:

Agency   Change of Heart   Consecration & Sacrifice   Dating Decisions
Dependability   Eternal Perspective   Eternal Life   Family Activities
Family (extended)   Families (eternal)   Family Unity
Friendships   Forgiveness   Healthy Habits   Heavenly Father   Heritage
Homemaking   Honesty   Individual Worth   Jesus Christ   Love
Marriage Standards   Missionary Service   Missionary Work
Money Management   Obedience   Opposition   Planning
Preparing for Change   Priesthood   Priesthood Blessings   Prophets
Purpose in Life   Repentance   Restoration   Righteousness   Scripture Study
Service in Community   Service in Church   Standards   Teaching
Temple Endowment   Temple Marriage   Temple Preparation   Vocation

Covenant Communications, Inc.
American Fork, Utah

Printed in the United States of America
First Printing: July 1998

Young Women FUN-TASTIC! Activities - Manual 3

ISBN 1-57734-298-4

ACKNOWLEDGMENTS: Thanks to Inspire Graphics, Inc. for the use of Lettering Delights computer fonts.

Meet the Creators of this Young Women Fun-tastic! Activities and Many Popular Creative Teaching Tools

Mary H. Ross Author and
Jennette Guymon-King, Illustrator
are the creators of

PRIMARY PARTNERS: *Lesson Activities to Make Learning Fun for:*
Nursery and Age 3 (Sunbeams)—Vol. 1 and II
CTR A and CTR B Ages 4-7
Book of Mormon Ages 8-11
Doctrine & Covenants/Church History Ages 8-11
Old Testament and New Testament Ages 8-11
Achievement Days, Girls Ages 8-11
Look for PRIMARY PARTNERS on CD-ROM

FAMILY HOME EVENING BOOKS:
Home-spun Fun FAMILY HOME EVENINGS
File Folder FAMILY HOME EVENINGS

MARY H. ROSS, *Author*
Mary Ross is an energetic mother, Primary teacher, and has been an Achievement Days leader. She loves to help children have a good time while they learn. She has studied acting, modeling, and voice. Her varied interests include writing, creating activities and children's parties, and cooking. Mary and her husband, Paul, live with their daughter, Jennifer, in Sandy, Utah

JENNETTE GUYMON-KING,
Illustrator
Jennette Guymon-King has studied graphic arts and illustration at Utah Valley State College and the University of Utah. She is currently employed with a commercial construction company. She served a mission to Japan. Jennette enjoys sports, reading, cooking, art, gardening, and freelance illustrating. Jennette and her husband, Clayton, live in Riverton, Utah.

My Young Women
Value-able Journal

photo

I will bloom
where I'm planted.

"Thou shalt be like a watered garden."
Isaiah 58:2-14

INTRODUCTION
Fun-tastic! Young Women Activities:
Lesson Lifesavers and More for Manual 3*

Young Women leaders, you'll find the following activities
to match lessons #1-47 to help young women
"Bloom Where They Are Planted."

❀ Lesson Activities   ❀ Midweek Activities
❀ Thought Treats   ❀ Scripture Cards
❀ Young Woman's Journal with
7 Value Divider Tabs to Store Activities
❀ 7 Floral Symbols to Identify Values

❀ Many of the midweek activities in this book were contributed by Fern
Law, a Young Women leader of six years. Her comments about the book:
*"The activities in this book focus on Jesus Christ and his gospel. They will
encourage young woman to search within themselves and feel deeply the
love and devotion of their Savior, and to be a light unto the world."*

How to Use This Book:

❀ <u>**Lessons #1-47 Table of Contents**</u> helps you locate lesson
activities quickly.

❀ <u>**A-Z Table of Contents**</u> helps you locate activities by subject.

❀ <u>**Lesson Activities**</u> coordinate with
specific parts of the lesson (for
example, Lesson #5 Home-making
Happy Habits Quiz compliments page
17 in the Young Women Manual,
shown right).

Review *"A Young Woman Creates a
Mood in Her Home"* writing section
(page 17) in Young Women Manual.

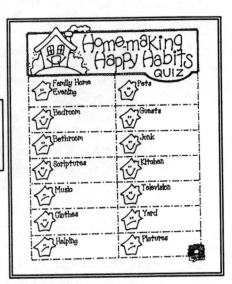

❀ <u>**Midweek Activities**</u> add to and enhance your lessons with a
lesson follow-up activity during the next week. This keeps the
subject open for discussion, giving more meaning to the lesson taught
on Sunday. IDEA: Use the first 10-15 minutes of your
midweek activity to present a lesson match midweek
activity. Many of the midweek activity ideas can take up
the entire evening.

❀ <u>**Scripture Cards**</u> (pages 108-123)
encourage young women to learn a value-able
scripture each week. Fill in the blanks and
color the floral symbol.

My Testimony Grows as I Study the Scriptures

OPPOSITION Can Make Me Strong

D&C 121:7-8 "My son, peace be unto thy soul; thine
_ _ _ _ _ _ _ _ _ and thine
afflictions shall be but a small moment.
And then, if thou _ _ _ _ _ _ _ _ it well,
God shall exalt thee on high; thou shalt
triumph over all thy foes."

Young Woman Value: Integrity (purple pansy) Lesson #23 Manual 3

*Young Women Manual 3 and Personal Progress is published by The Church of Jesus Christ of Latter-day Saints, Salt Lake City, Utah.

❀ **Personal Progress* Goals** are cross referenced with each week's lesson. To motivate goal achievement, spotlight young women who have achieved these specific goals, having them share their experiences.

❀ **ORGANIZE JOURNAL AND ACTIVITIES.**
1. Set Up Journals. Help young women set up their journal. Select a three-ring binder for each young woman. Copy the seven value cover pages and value tabs (on the pages that follow).

2. Identify Floral Symbols. The floral symbols (shown above) found on the activities and scripture cards will help young women identify the values: Faith (white lily), Choice & Accountability (orange poppy), Good Works (yellow sunflower), Integrity (purple pansy), Knowledge (green ivy), Divine Nature (blue morning glory), and Individual Worth (red rose).

3. Color-Code Journal by coloring the floral symbol hidden on most of the activities (shown right). Paper punch activity page, and place activity in journal binder behind the value tab. Encourage young women to post the activity to review during the week before placing activity in their journal. POCKETS: Place pockets on the back of journal pages by cutting paper in thirds and gluing 1/4" on bottom and sides. Place odd sized activities in pockets.

❀ **Thought Treats** teach lesson concepts (when appropriate). Many treats can be delivered during the week or used during midweek activities to reinforce gospel learning. Attach motivational notes to treats, e.g. Lesson #1 "Crown Cookies." NOTE IDEA:

"Here's a CELESTIAL CROWN COOKIE to remind you that you are a princess in Heavenly Father's kingdom."

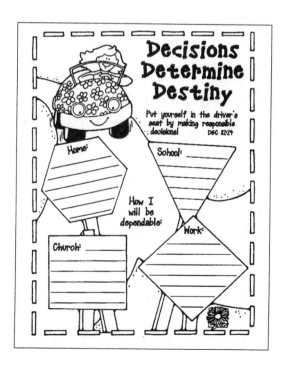

❀ **Evening of Excellence** is a great time for young women to display their Young Woman's Value-able Journal. Each week they can collect activities and handouts and store in their journal. Parents will delight in their daughters' grasp of gospel subjects. Girls can also display their scrapbooks and Personal Progress journals.

❀ At **General Conference** time, present the activity from lesson #47 (pages 106-107).

TABLE OF CONTENTS
Young Women FUN-TASTIC! ACTIVITIES - Manual 3

Young Women Manual 3 is published by The Church of Jesus Christ of Latter-day Saints, Salt Lake City, Utah.

TABLE OF CONTENTS
Young Women FUN-TASTIC! ACTIVITIES - Manual 3

*Young Women Manual 3 is published by The Church of Jesus Christ of Latter-day Saints, Salt Lake City, Utah.

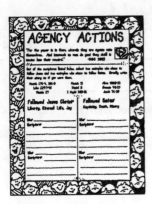

AGENCY: I Will Follow Jesus Christ
(Agency Actions cross match) 55-56

CHANGE OF HEART: I Will Be
Faithful (Change of Heart mobile) . . 65-67

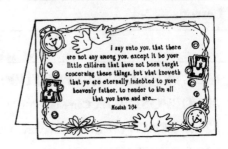

CONSECRATION: I Will Sacrifice
(Time, Talents, Means tent card) . . 63-64

DATING DECISIONS Affect Eternal Life
(Big Dating Decisions poster) 80-82

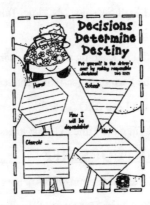

DEPENDABILITY: I Will Be
Dependable (Destiny planner) 94-95

ETERNAL PERSPECTIVE: Facing
Trials ("Bee" Eternally motivators) . 49-50

ETERNAL LIFE: I Can Obtain (Eternal
Life word find) 34-35

FAMILY ACTIVITIES:
(Family Fun Activity Sack) 20-23

FAMILY: Being Friends with Extended
Family (closeness checklist/postcard) 24-25

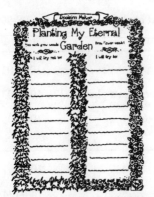

FAMILIES: Worthy of Eternal Blessings
(My Eternal Garden decision maker) 16-17

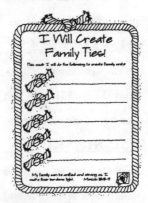

FAMILY UNITY: Creating Family Ties
(family unity checklist) 18-19

FRIENDSHIP: Each Is Divine and Eternal
(Friend-"ship" Anchors) 75-77

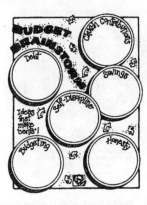

RIGHTEOUSNESS: Draw Close to the Savior (Warm Fuzzy mirror motivator)   6-7

SCRIPTURE STUDY: I Love to Read the Scriptures (bookmark/journal) 68-69

SERVICE IN COMMUNITY: Time for Others (Service Project Planner) 73-74

SERVICE IN CHURCH: Serve the Lord (L.D.S. PRESS interview tools) 70-72

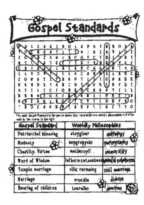

STANDARDS: World Philosophies (Gospel Standards word find) 85-86

TEACHING: Follow Example of Jesus (Teaching Talents and Tools journal) 12-13

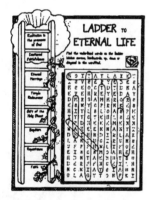

TEMPLE ENDOWMENT: (Ladder to Eternal Life word search) 36-37

TEMPLE MARRIAGE: Prepare (Smooth Sailing Companion-"ship" journal) . . . 8-9

TEMPLE MARRIAGE: Together Forever (Sacred Triangle mobile) . . . 40-42

TEMPLE MARRIAGE: Mr. and Mrs. Promises (M&M Thought Treat) . . 40, 42

TEMPLE PREPARATION: Prepare to Enter (temple scripture clue puzzle). . 38-39

VOCATION: Choose Vocation Wisely (Give a Hoot! future focus planner) 102-103

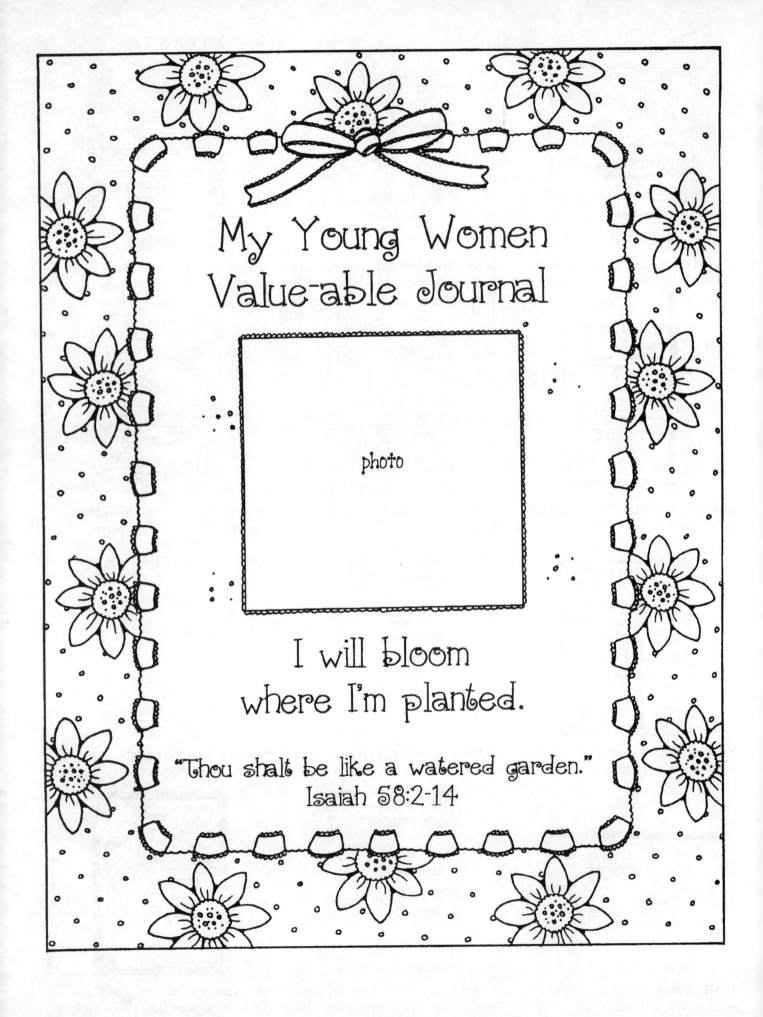

My Young Women Value-able Journal

photo

I will bloom
where I'm planted.

"Thou shalt be like a watered garden."
Isaiah 58:2-14

Divider Tabs for Young Women Value-able Journal

HOW TO PLACE TABS ON DIVIDER SHEETS:
1. Copy tabs on white cardstock paper.
2. Color floral symbols: Faith (white), Divine Nature (blue), Individual Worth (red), Knowledge (green), Choice & Accountability (orange), Good Works (yellow), and Integrity (purple).
3. Cover with clear contact paper to reinforce tabs.
4. Cut out and fold above word line, i.e. fold above "Faith."
5. Glue or tape tab on divider page in order of the five values.
6. You will also find tabs for Calendar, Family Home Evening, Friends, Personal Progress, and Notes

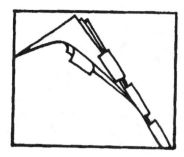

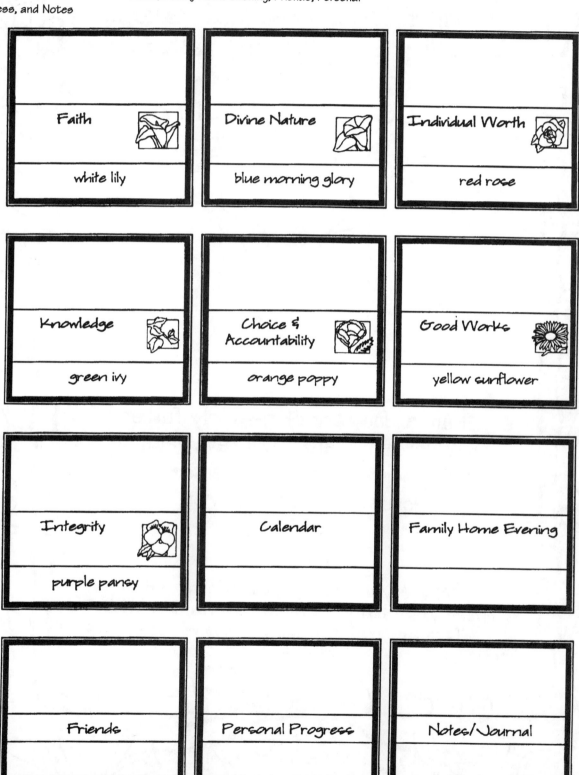

Faith — white lily

Divine Nature — blue morning glory

Individual Worth — red rose

Knowledge — green ivy

Choice & Accountability — orange poppy

Good Works — yellow sunflower

Integrity — purple pansy

Calendar

Family Home Evening

Friends

Personal Progress

Notes/Journal

I Am of Great Worth and Value ...
According to My Heavenly Father Who
Knows Me Perfectly

Value: Faith

(white lily)

"I am a daughter of Heavenly Father
who loves me, and I will have faith in
his eternal plan, which centers in
Jesus Christ, my Savior."

"And, if you keep my commandments and
endure to the end you shall have eternal life, which
gift is the greatest of all the gifts of God."
D&C 14:17

I Am of Great Worth and Value ...
According to My Heavenly Father Who
Knows Me Perfectly

Value: Divine Nature

(blue morning glory)

"I have inherited divine qualities
which I will strive to develop."

"Be partakers of the divine nature, ...
giving all diligence, add to your faith virtue; and to
virtue knowledge: And to knowledge temperance:
and to temperance patience: and to patience
godliness: And to godliness brotherly kindness;
and to brotherly kindness charity."
2 Peter 1:4-7

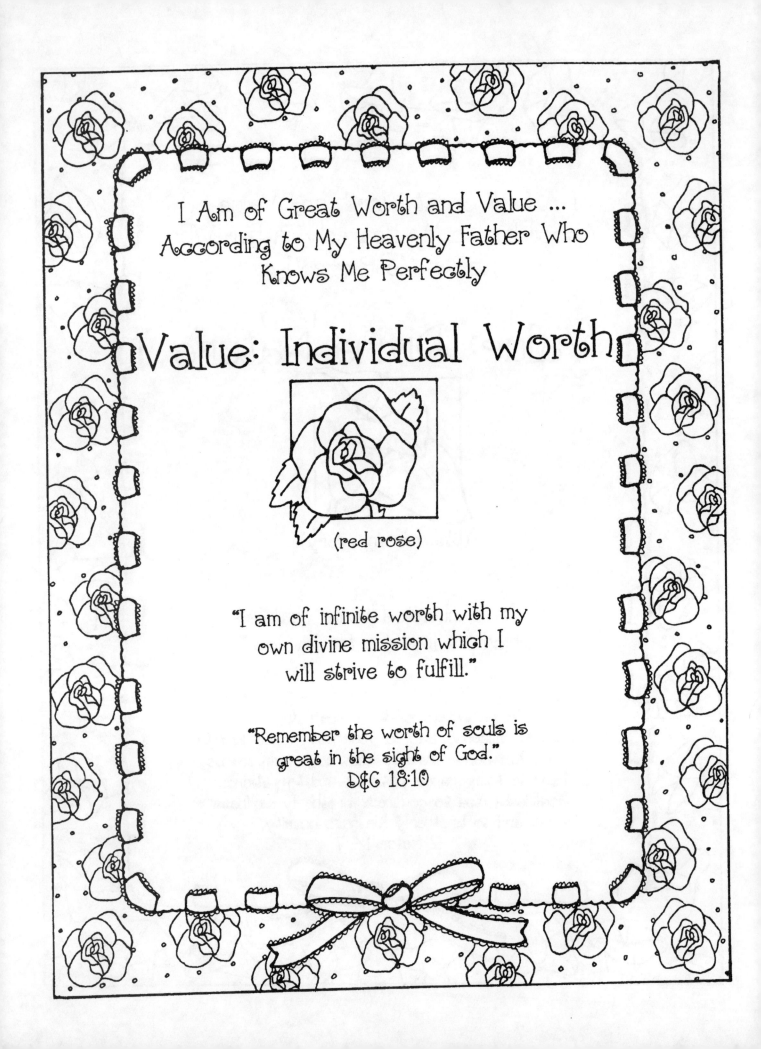

I Am of Great Worth and Value ...
According to My Heavenly Father Who
Knows Me Perfectly

Value: Individual Worth

(red rose)

"I am of infinite worth with my
own divine mission which I
will strive to fulfill."

"Remember the worth of souls is
great in the sight of God."
D&C 18:10

I Am of Great Worth and Value ...
According to My Heavenly Father Who
Knows Me Perfectly

Value: Knowledge

(green ivy)

"I will continually seek
opportunities for learning
and growth."

"Seek learning, even by study
and also by faith."
D&C 88:118

I Am of Great Worth and Value ...
According to My Heavenly Father Who
Knows Me Perfectly

Value: Choice & Accountability

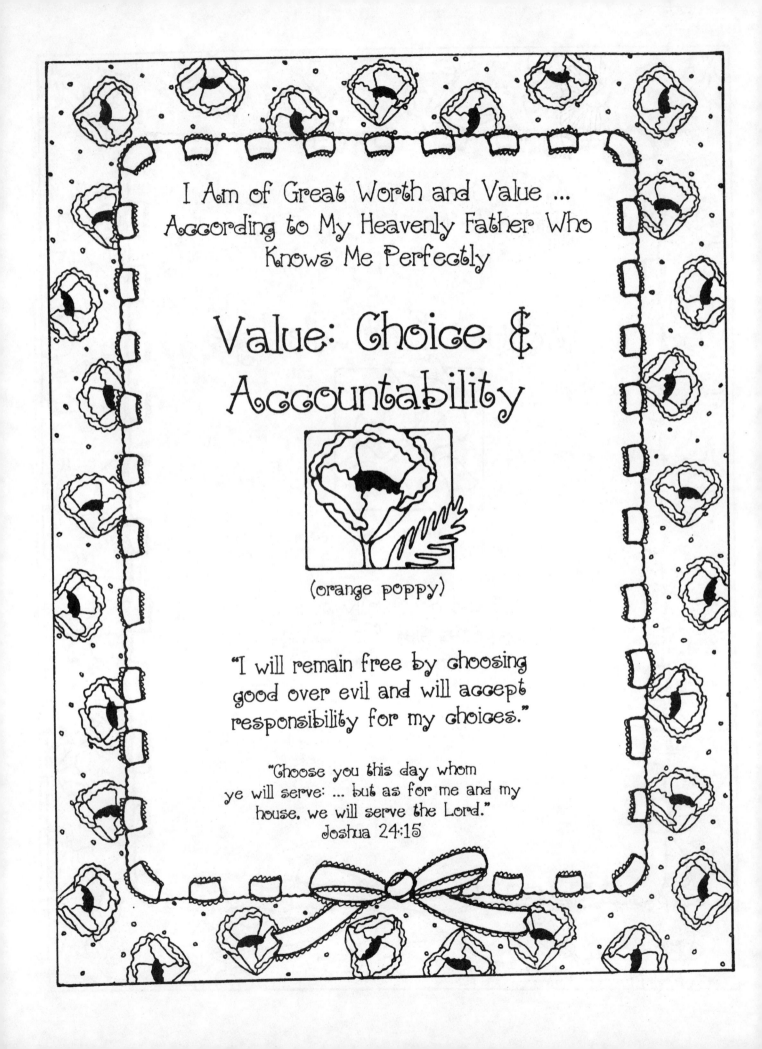

(orange poppy)

"I will remain free by choosing
good over evil and will accept
responsibility for my choices."

"Choose you this day whom
ye will serve: ... but as for me and my
house, we will serve the Lord."
Joshua 24:15

I Am of Great Worth and Value ...
According to My Heavenly Father Who
Knows Me Perfectly

Value: Good Works

(yellow sunflower)

"I will nurture others and build the
kingdom through righteous service."

"Therefore let your light so shine
before this people, that they may see your good
works and glorify your father who is in heaven."
3 Nephi 12:16

I Am of Great Worth and Value ...
According to My Heavenly Father Who
Knows Me Perfectly

Value: Integrity

(purple pansy)

"I will have the moral courage to
make my actions consistent
with my knowledge of right
and wrong."

"Till I die I will not remove
mine integrity from me."
Job 27:5

Lesson #1	**HEAVENLY FATHER:** I Am a Daughter of God
	(scripture search journal)

YOU'LL NEED: Copy of a scripture search journal (page 2) on colored cardstock paper for each young woman, pencils, and colored markers.

ACTIVITY: Help young women discover the attributes of God, our Heavenly Father, by reading the scriptures and filling in the missing words. Then help young women write their thoughts about these scriptures.

Review Chalkboard or poster presentation (page 3) in Young Women Manual 3*.

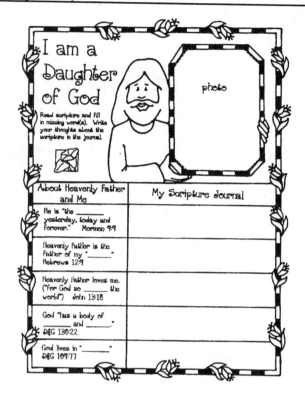

2. Tell young women that when they learn about Jesus Christ, they learn about Heavenly Father and the Holy Ghost, because the members of the Godhead are *one* in a purpose, even though they are *three* separate beings (John 17:20-23).
3. Ahead of time collect recent wallet size photos of each young woman to insert into the frame. Cut slits in the page along the four sides of the frames to insert picture.

COLOR SYMBOL: Color floral symbol on activity and scripture card. File activity in Young Women Value-able Journal behind the value tab.

Divine Nature (blue morning glory)

PERSONAL PROGRESS* GOALS:
Beehive 1 (Faith 6, Individual Worth 8),
Beehive 2 (Faith 7), Mia Maid 1 (Faith 1, 4, 9)

THOUGHT TREAT: Crown Cookies.
(1) Cut out sugar cookie dough into crown shapes.
(2) Bake and glaze with vanilla frosting glaze (dilute frosting until runny, then apply with a pastry brush).
(3) Place jelly beans on top to represent crown jewels. (4) Share cookies and tell young women that because God is our Heavenly Father, and we are his daughters, we are of royal descent. We are princesses in his kingdom and have the potential to become goddesses in the celestial kingdom.

MIDWEEK ACTIVITIES:
Royalty Procession. Invite the parents to enjoy this evening. Roll out the red carpet (red butcher paper) and honor young women for their desire to obey the commandments and obtain the celestial kingdom. Place red paper (for carpet) in the center aisle between the chairs where the parents are seated. Ahead of time: Outline the commandments we are asked to live in order to become queens in the celestial kingdom. Create a 10" x 5' royalty bandelo that streams over their right shoulder and over their back. Make bandelo out of butcher paper (in a variety of bright colors). Option: Enlarge jewels from this book to place on bandelos or crowns. Write the commandments on the front. Make up a script for each young woman to read after she formally walks up the red carpet to the front. The script would tell about the commandment she is representing, e.g.: *"I am of royal blood, a princess in Heavenly Father's kingdom. I will honor my parents. I will seek for their guidance. I will listen to their counsel as they guide me in righteousness. I will care for them when they are old."* After the young woman's speech, place a crown on her head. Give her a silk flower (that represents one of the values).

I Am a Daughter of God

Read scripture and fill in missing word(s). Write your thoughts about the scripture in the journal.

photo

About Heavenly Father and Me	My Scripture Journal
He is "the _____ yesterday, today and forever." Mormon 9:9	
Heavenly Father is the father of my "_____" Hebrews 12:9	
Heavenly Father loves me. ("for God so _____ the world") John 13:18	
God "has a body of _____ and _____." D&C 130:22	
God lives in "_____" D&C 109:77	

Lesson #2	**JESUS CHRIST:** I Will Think of My Savior
	(What Think Ye of Christ? journal and cards)

YOU'LL NEED: Copy two journal pages and 1 set of ponder cards (pages 4-5) for each young woman, pencils, and colored markers.

ACTIVITY:

> *Review Testimony (page 8) in Young Women Manual 3**

1. Journal #1. Give young women one journal page and ask them to write what they think of their Savior, Jesus Christ. Make sure they enter the date.

2. Ponder Cards. Cut out ahead of time and give them a set of scripture cards. Ask them to search and ponder these scriptures and write what they think of Jesus Christ on each card, as it pertains to the scripture.

3. Journal #2. About 2 months later or after they have completed the Savior ponder cards (#2 above), do the following: Give young women the second journal page "What think ye of Christ?" and ask young women to again write their feelings about the Savior. Have them date this journal page. Then compare the two testimonies. There will be a difference.

4. Follow with a testimony meeting.

5. Explain that they can draw closer to their Savior, opening the door to let him help them in their lives by following the four steps outlined in the lesson (see Summary page 8).

COLOR SYMBOL: Color floral symbol on activity and scripture card. File activity in Young Women Value-able Journal behind the value tab.

Faith (white lily)

PERSONAL PROGRESS* GOALS:
Beehive 1 (Divine Nature 3), Beehive 2 (Faith 4), Mia Maid 1 (Faith 7, 8, Divine Nature 1, 6), Mia Maid 2 (Faith 3, Divine Nature 3, 4, Integrity 5)

THOUGHT TREAT: Graham Cracker Doors. Frost (glue) a round Dots candy or jelly bean on the right center of a large graham

cracker to look like a door. As young women eat their cracker door, talk about things they have done or someone else has done to open the door or draw closer to the Savior.

MIDWEEK ACTIVITIES:

1. **Walk Where Jesus Walked.** Have someone who has been to the Holy Land, come and tell where Jesus walked and what he did. Or, go through the New Testament and Book of Mormon to see where Jesus walked, asking each young woman to take a specific story to present in chronological order, spotlighting the life of Jesus. Encourage young women to take these home and present during family home evening. See *File Folder Family Home Evenings (New Testament)*, created by Mary Ross and Jennette Guymon-King.

2. **Book Reviews of Jesus Christ.** Have young women take their favorite chapter of their family's favorite LDS book about Jesus Christ. Give each young women 5 minutes to tell about the chapter. List the reading material for each young woman to place in their journal behind the Divine Nature tab. Book Ideas: *Jesus the Christ, Believing in Christ, Faith Proceeds the Miracle*, and other books by latter-day prophets and General Authorities.

What think ye of Christ?

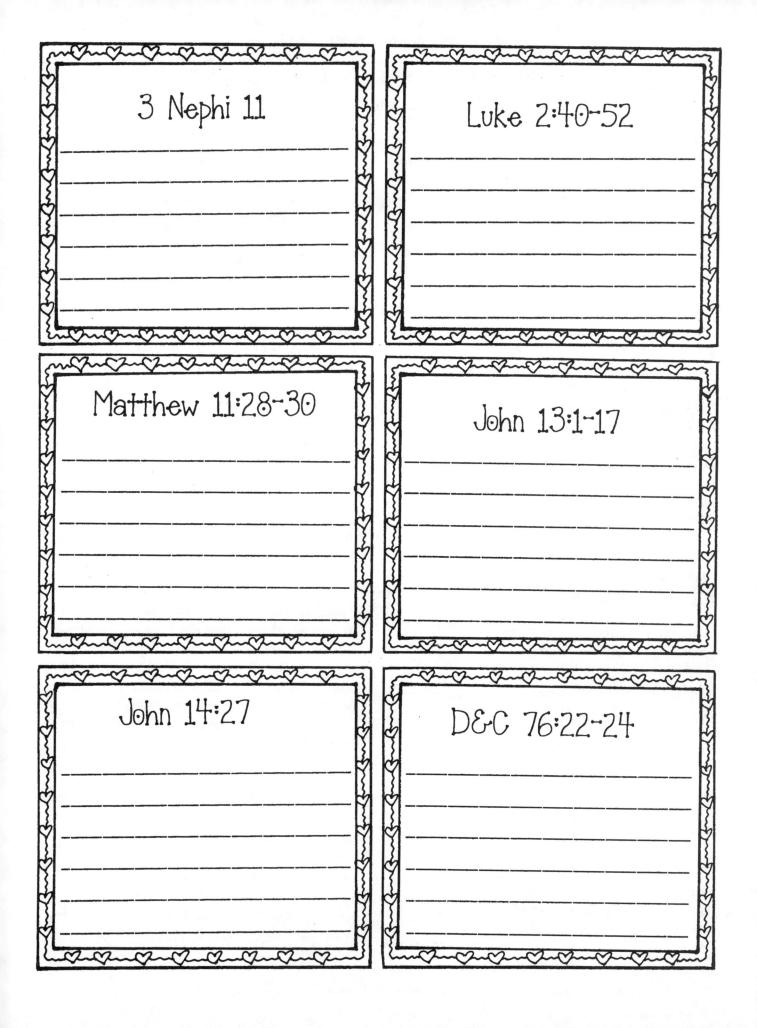

3 Nephi 11

Luke 2:40-52

Matthew 11:28-30

John 13:1-17

John 14:27

D&C 76:22-24

Lesson #3*   **RIGHTEOUSNESS: I Will Draw Close to the Savior**
(service bookmark, and Warm Fuzzy mirror motivator)

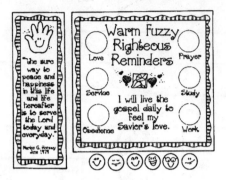

YOU'LL NEED: Copy of bookmark and Warm Fuzzy mirror motivator (page 7) on colored cardstock paper, six cotton balls or colored pom-poms for each young woman, and scissors, glue, and colored markers.

ACTIVITY:

Review Chalkboard discussion and wordstrips (page 9-10) and Quotation (page 10) in Young Women Manual 3*.

1. Color and cut out bookmark, reminding us that we can draw close to the Savior by serving him everyday.

2. Create a mirror motivator, a Warm Fuzzy Righteous Reminder to remind us of the six ways we can feel close to the Savior each day.

TO CREATE MIRROR MOTIVATOR:

1. Color and cut out reminder, leaving happy face glue-on stickers attached.

2. Glue six colored cotton balls or pom-poms above the six challenges: Love, prayer, service, obedience, study, and work. Ask young women to share their thoughts about each challenge.

3. Ask young women to post this on their mirror during the week to read and try to live these six challenges every day. As they do, they can cut out a smile sticker and glue the sticker on the pom-pom as a reward.

COLOR SYMBOL: Color floral symbol on activity and scripture card. File activity in Young Women Value-able Journal behind the value tab.

Divine Nature (blue morning glory)

PERSONAL PROGRESS* GOALS:

Beehive 1 (Integrity 3, 4, 5),
Beehive 2 (Divine Nature 1, Integrity 5, 8),
Mia Maid 1 (Knowledge 6, Integrity 7),
Mia Maid 2 (Faith 5, 7, Divine Nature 5, Individual Worth 3, Integrity 1, 3, 6)

THOUGHT TREAT: Warm Fuzzy Fizzies. Give each young woman a can of fizzy soda pop to sip as they tell you about the warm feelings they receive when they make a right choice.

MIDWEEK ACTIVITIES:

1. **Small Acts of Kindness.** Brainstorm and write down to preserve in a file for each young woman, a list of small acts of kindness they can do for others. Encourage them to look into the mirror and say, "Mirror, mirror, tell me true. Is His image in my countenance, too?" As they say this, they can look at the list and perform small acts of kindness. IDEAS: ☺ A sweet anonymous note ☺ A phone call to someone less active ☺ A smile, ☺ Breakfast in bed for a family member ☺ A friendly touch ☺ A compliment ☺ Find out someone's favorite goody, make it for them, and deliver with a smile.

2. **Happiness Gifts.** Ask young women and leaders to share ideas on how they can be happy by serving others. Place a gift box on the table, labeled, "Happiness is a gift I can give myself, as I serve others." Cut a hole in the back of the gift box (or lift the lid) to fill with names of those participating. Draw names from the box to present their ideas. Assign several scriptures to read that tell ways to be happy through service: 1 Nephi 8:10, 2 Nephi 2:13, Mosiah 2:17, 2:41, Mosiah 16:11, Alma 3:26, 27:18, 41:5, 10, 4 Nephi 1:15, D&C 4:2, 76:5. IDEAS: Balance your life with personal care and selfless care (serving others). Focus on grooming self and taking care of personal needs quickly, then spend time serving others. This selfless act of taking your mind off yourself and focusing on others will bring a lasting joy that does not come from self-focus (being wrapped up in yourself).

Warm Fuzzy
Righteous
Reminders

Prayer

Study

Work

Love

Service

Obedience

I will live the gospel daily to feel my Savior's love.

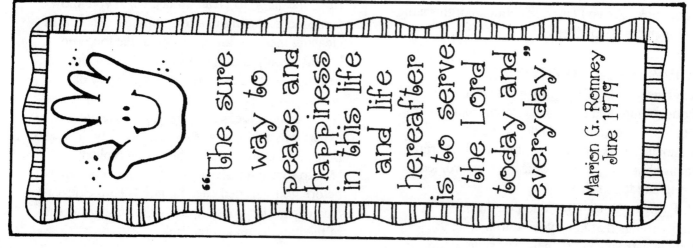

"The sure way to peace and happiness in this life and life hereafter is to serve the Lord today and everyday."

Marion G. Romney
June 1979

Lesson #4*	**TEMPLE MARRIAGE:** I Will Prepare to Be an Eternal Companion
	(Smooth Sailing Companion-"ship" journal)

YOU'LL NEED: Copy of journal (page 9) for each young woman, pencils, and colored markers.

ACTIVITY:
Help young women think of what they can do now to prepare to be an eternal companion. Write ideas on this Smooth Sailing Companion-"ship" journal page.

> *Review Preparation #2 (page 14), and Lesson Application (page 16) in Young Women Manual 3*.*

IDEAS: ❤ study scriptures often ❤ have family home evening regularly ❤ listen ❤ share skills with young children ❤ cook basic healthy balanced meals ❤ babysit ❤ practice housekeeping skills ❤ balance a checkbook ❤ budget money ❤ be a good friend ❤ share ❤ smile and look on the bright side ❤ learn to can produce ❤ learn to sew ❤ learn gardening skills ❤ save money for a rainy day ❤ cook up a storm, but don't let the dishes reign ❤ clean house before bed ❤ plan clothing before bed

COLOR SYMBOL: Color floral symbol on activity and scripture card. File activity in Young Women Value Journal behind the value tab.

Divine Nature (blue morning glory)

THOUGHT TREAT: Companion-ship Sandwich. Make a half sandwich for each young woman and place a cheese sail on top with a toothpick. As you eat, talk about smooth sailing companion-"ship" ideas.

MIDWEEK ACTIVITIES:
1. Organize Don't Agonize. Have a very good housekeeper and homemaker come and talk to young women about schedules, especially balancing work and family time. Collect bright ideas about organizing, or ask young women to bring an idea to share.
2. Pamper Yourself. "Sharpen the saw," by doing things that keep your spirits up, e.g., bubble bath, manicure, new hair style, good

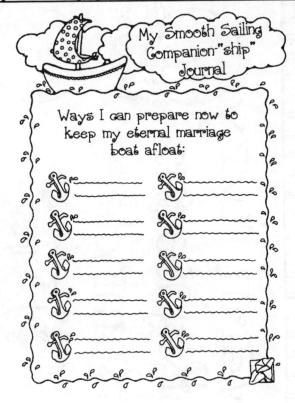

My Smooth Sailing Companion-"ship" Journal

Ways I can prepare now to keep my eternal marriage boat afloat:

book, prayer, walks, grooming, uplifting scriptures.
3. Guest Pretend. Have young women organize and do a guest pretend (anticipate a visitor and clean the house and perk up your image). Choose one day the next week and help young women create a list of what needs to be done in order to make their home presentable for a very important guest.

It's too easy to "sweep the dirt under the rug," meaning, to clean up fast when you know someone is coming in a few minutes. This crash cleaning method doesn't work in the long run, because you put things away where they don't belong, which adds to the stress of every day living.

Collect ideas to share, e.g., a cleaning expert was asked how she controls dirty dishes so they don't clutter the kitchen. She replied, "Make sure the dishwasher is run and emptied before going to bed each night. Then the next day, every dish goes into the dish washer instead of the counter and in the sink."

Young Women Manual 3 and Personal Progress books are published by The Church of Jesus Christ of Latter-day Saints, Salt Lake City, Utah.

My Smooth Sailing
Companion-"ship"
Journal

Ways I can prepare now to
keep my eternal marriage
boat afloat:

Lesson #5*	Homemaking: I Will Create a Spiritual Environment in My Home
	("Home"-making Happy Habits Quiz)

YOU'LL NEED: Copy of quiz (page 11) for each young woman, scissor, pencils, and markers.

ACTIVITY: Help young women analyze their current physical environment and habits, to see where they will be in the future in their own home.

> Review "A Woman Creates a Mood in Her Home" writing section (page 17) in Young Women Manual 3*.

Remind them that "home"-making habits start early, but it's not too late to develop new habits that can create happiness in your home now and later.

1. Take the "Home"-making Happy Habits Quiz. HERE'S HOW: Go from room to room or habit to habit (thinking about your homemaking habits you have now). Write in the frowns what you will do to change a bad habit in that room or action (music, scriptures). Write in the smiles ways you can improve an already good situation.

2. Ask young women what habits they would give up each day to replace them with happy habits. Write these on the back of quiz.

3. Tell young women that when their environment (home) is cluttered and disorganized, their mind tends to be cluttered and disorganized. Environment affects how we think and feel about ourselves.

COLOR SYMBOL: Color floral symbol on activity and scripture card. File activity in Young Women Value-able Journal behind the value tab.

Good Works (yellow sunflower)

PERSONAL PROGRESS* GOALS:
Beehive 1 (Good Works 4),
Mia Maid 1 (Choice & Accountability 5)

THOUGHT TREAT:
Happy Home Gingerbread Cookie. Cut out a house shape out of gingerbread dough. Decorate house with frosting and candies, or frost a happy smile on each cookie. Ask young women and leaders to share home-making happy habits.

MIDWEEK ACTIVITIES:
IDEA #1: Room-Make-over. Ask several young women to volunteer and have a drawing for choices #1 and #2 (below). Obtain parents' permission before doing these, coordinating efforts with those who share a room.
Choice #1: Free Room Face Lift: Have the young women come to this lucky young woman's room to wash windows, vacuum, rearrange furniture, closets, drawers, and desk. Choice #2: Room Show: Ask young women ahead of time to show the others their room, sharing ideas on how they organize and create a wholesome atmosphere.
WHOLESOME ROOM ATMOSPHERE IDEAS:
Have the *Era* and *Ensign* magazines, scriptures, and other spiritual uplifting books in your room. Have music that is uplifting and invites the Spirit. Post spiritual messages, young women handouts, and MORMONAD posters. Know that a room well groomed and functional is a room that can enhance spiritual growth. How you keep your room now reflects on your future home. Home is where your heart is. Put your heart into designing a room where peace can abide.
IDEA #2: Home-making Hint Box or Journal.
Create a box or journal pockets and pages to collect hints to make the home a clean and spiritual environment. Share some from magazines, e.g., how to enjoy evening meals and conversation.

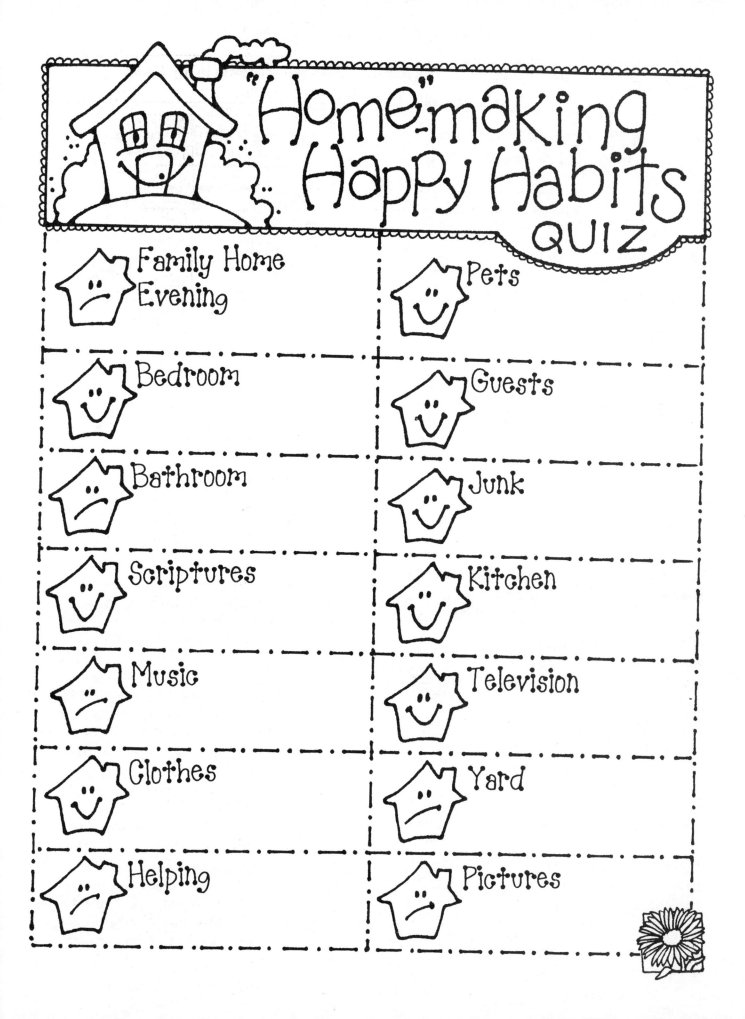

"Home"-making Happy Habits QUIZ

Family Home Evening

Pets

Bedroom

Guests

Bathroom

Junk

Scriptures

Kitchen

Music

Television

Clothes

Yard

Helping

Pictures

Lesson #6*	**TEACHING:** I Will Follow the Example of Jesus
	(Teaching Talents and Tools journal)

YOU'LL NEED: Copy of teaching journal (page 13) for each young woman, pencils, and colored markers.

ACTIVITY:

> *Review Teacher presentation "Jesus Christ Is Our Example as a Teacher" and scriptures and discussion (pages 21-22) in Young Women Manual 3*.*

Help young women learn to follow the Savior's example when they teach. Use this journal of Teaching Talents and Tools to help them plan their next teaching assignment. Coordinate an opportunity for the young women to teach Primary (e.g., while Relief Society and priesthood meet together in a joint meeting). Talk about the tools that Jesus used when he taught (found in the border). Help young women plan, carry out, and have a positive teaching experience. If teaching opportunities are not available, young women could use this to prepare and carry out a family home evening presentation.

COLOR SYMBOL: Color floral symbol on activity and scripture card. File activity in Young Women Value-able Journal behind the value tab.

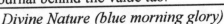

Divine Nature (blue morning glory)

PERSONAL PROGRESS* GOALS:
Beehive 1 (Divine Nature 3),
Mia Maid 1 (Integrity 8), Laurel 1 & 2 Project #2 (page 79)

THOUGHT TREAT: Teach with the Spirit Marshmellow Holy Ghosts. Attach two large marshmellows on a toothpick for each young woman. While eating, talk about how young women feel when a lesson is taught by the Spirit and one that does not invite the Spirit. Ask them, to think about actions in their daily lives; which actions invite the Spirit and which actions turn it away?

MIDWEEK ACTIVITIES:
1. **Panel Discussion** with LDS teachers who teach with the Spirit. People on the panel should

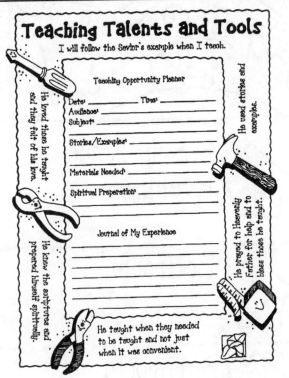

Teaching Talents and Tools
I will follow the Savior's example when I teach.

He loved those he taught and they felt of his love.

He used stories and examples.

Teaching Opportunity Planner

Date: _____ Time: _____
Audience: _____
Subject: _____

Stories/Examples: _____

Materials Needed: _____

Spiritual Preparation: _____

He prayed to Heavenly Father for help and to bless those he taught.

He knew the scriptures and prepared himself spiritually.

Journal of My Experience
_____
_____
_____
_____
_____

He taught when they needed to be taught and not just when it was convenient.

understand the importance of having the Spirit. Examples: A few mothers, a few young women, a bishopric member, a seminary teacher, etc.

Point #1: Talk about moments of having the Holy Ghost and being an effective teacher, and not having the Holy Ghost and being an ineffective teacher.

Point #2: Present a conference talk such as President Holland's Saturday session of the May 1998 *Ensign*, or others on teaching. Help young women understand that anyone can teach if they have the Spirit, and anyone can fail to teach if the Spirit is not there.

Point #3: Talk about key scriptures, e.g., "If ye have not the Spirit, ye shall not teach" (D&C 42:14). Others: Alma 18:34, Moroni 10:9-10, D&C 36:2, 43:15, 50:14.

Point #4: Have young women write ahead of time questions they wish to ask the panel, e.g., How do you teach a child who is not willing to listen, a child who is not reverent? How do you help children gain a desire to study the scriptures? How do you help a child make choices by listening to the Spirit of the Holy Ghost?

 *Young Women Manual 3 and Personal Progress books are published by The Church of Jesus Christ of Latter-day Saints, Salt Lake City, Utah.

Teaching Talents and Tools

I will follow the Savior's example when I teach.

Teaching Opportunity Planner

Date: _____ Time: _____

Audience: _____

Subject: _____

_____

Stories/Examples: _____

_____

_____

Materials Needed: _____

Spiritual Preparation: _____

_____

_____

Journal of My Experience

_____

_____

_____

_____

_____

_____

_____

He loved those he taught and they felt of his love.

He knew the scriptures and prepared himself spiritually.

He used stories and examples.

He prayed to Heavenly Father for help and to bless those he taught.

He taught when they needed to be taught and not just when it was convenient.

Lesson #7*

PURPOSE IN LIFE: I Will Tune into the Lord's Will
(My Righteous Radio teaching tool)

YOU'LL NEED: Copy of radio and arrow radio dial (page 15) on colored cardstock, OPTION: two buttons to glue on radio knobs for each young woman, scissors, razor blade, and markers.

ACTIVITY: Create a teaching tool to help young women review the five ways we can tune into the Lord's will: Personal prayer, study and meditation, gift of the Holy Ghost, priesthood blessings, and patriarchal blessings.

> *Review "Learning the Lord's Will Can Give Direction to Our Lives" discussion (page 24) in Young Women Manual 3*.*

Young women can tune into these on their own Righteous Radio as they read the poem and move the arrow dial back and forth.
1. Ahead of time, cut line above the word "RIGHTEOUS," with a razor blade.
2. OPTION: Glue or sew bottons on radio knobs.
3. Color and cut out radio and arrow.
4. Fold arrow as indicated.
5. Fit arrow into slit (see #1 above) and slide arrow dial back and forth. Tell young women, "As you are righteous, you can tune into the Lord's will and receive guidance throughout your life."
6. Young women can use their radios as a teaching tool to show their families in family home evening.

COLOR SYMBOL: Color floral symbol on activity and scripture card. File activity in Young Women Value-able Journal behind the value tab.

> *Faith (white lily)*

PERSONAL PROGRESS* GOALS:
Beehive 2 (Faith 7)

THOUGHT TREAT:
Graham Cracker Gumdrop Radio.
1. Press two gumdrops out flat with a rolling pin (rolled in sugar) to make radio knobs.
2. Glue gumdrop knobs on graham cracker (left and right bottom) with frosting.
3. Glue five gumdrops (or small candies) across top with frosting to represent the five radio stations.
4. Review the five ways shown above that we can tune into the Lord's will. Remind young women that one way they can tune in is through personal revelation that can only come through prayer, meditation, and the Gift of the Holy Ghost.

MIDWEEK ACTIVITIES:
1. Media Mania. Have an evening where a member of the bishopric or presidency of the Young Women present and discuss media, e.g., radio, television, satellite dish, cable, videos, Internet, and what to look for.
GOOD: Talk about the good things good media brings to our lives, e.g. values, beautiful music, genealogy research.
BAD: Then talk about self-control and mixed signals, Satan's design for the use of media. Parents can come.
RESEARCH: There are many articles available, e.g., "Reel Life vs. Real Life," by Joseph Walker, in the *Ensign*, June 1993, pages 15-19.
2. Tune-in Value-able List. Young women can create a list of uplifting videos, television shows, music, computer programs, Internet, and radio that express the Young Women values.

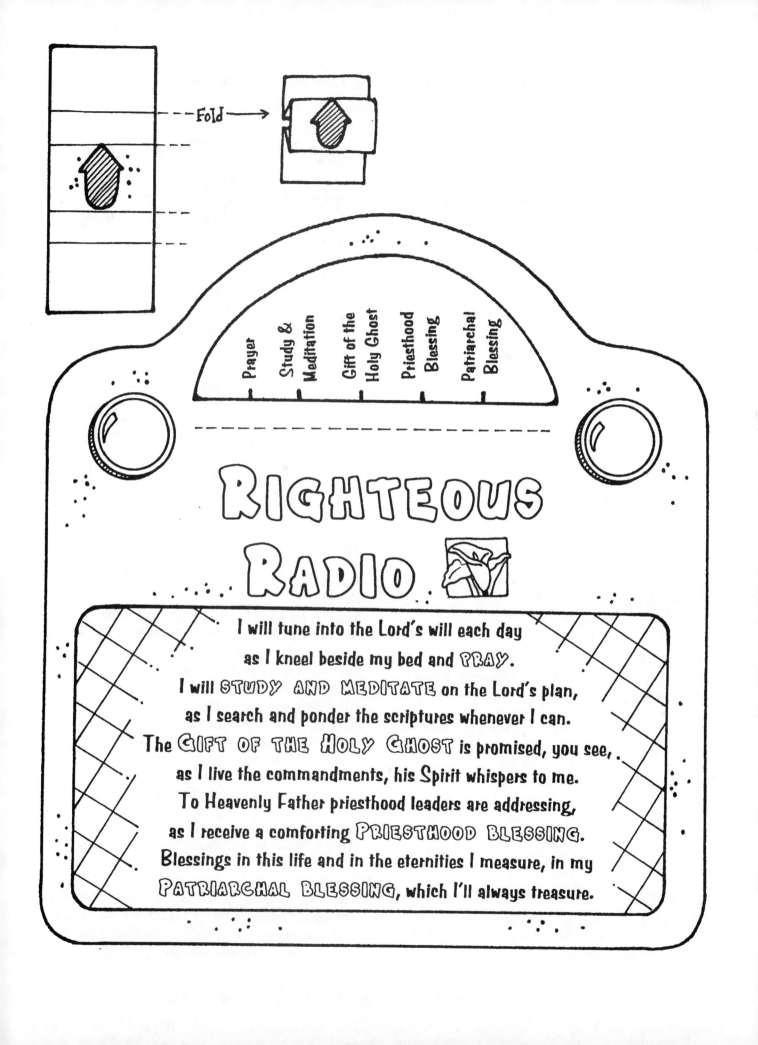

Fold →

Prayer

Study & Meditation

Gift of the Holy Ghost

Priesthood Blessing

Patriarchal Blessing

RIGHTEOUS RADIO

I will tune into the Lord's will each day
as I kneel beside my bed and PRAY.
I will STUDY AND MEDITATE on the Lord's plan,
as I search and ponder the scriptures whenever I can.
The GIFT OF THE HOLY GHOST is promised, you see,
as I live the commandments, his Spirit whispers to me.
To Heavenly Father priesthood leaders are addressing,
as I receive a comforting PRIESTHOOD BLESSING.
Blessings in this life and in the eternities I measure, in my
PATRIARCHAL BLESSING, which I'll always treasure.

Lesson #8*	FAMILIES (Eternal): I Will Be Worthy of Eternal Blessings
	(My Eternal Garden decision maker)

YOU'LL NEED: Copy of decision maker (page 17) for each young woman, pencils, and colored markers.

ACTIVITY: Help young women look at their life as an eternal garden that needs constant care.

> *Review Lesson Application (page 30) in Young Women Manual 3*.*

If we desire our family to be eternal, we must purposefully plant a flowerbed of beauty rather than a patch of noxious weeds. Decide what you will not grow in your eternal garden by listing things you will not do on the left. Decide what you will plant in your eternal garden by writing things you will try to do on the right. Tell young women they can be worthy of eternal blessings by making eternal decisions daily. Say, "Use this decision maker to plant eternal seeds within your mind, so you can grow beautiful flowers instead of noxious weeds."

COLOR SYMBOL: Color floral symbol on activity and scripture card. File activity in Young Women Value-able Journal behind the value tab.

Choice & Accountability (orange poppy)

PERSONAL PROGRESS* GOALS:
Beehive 1 (Divine Nature 8, Choice & Accountability 2), Beehive 2 (Individual Worth 7), Mia Maid 1 (Knowledge 8)

THOUGHT TREAT: OPTION #1: Smiling Sunflower Cookies. Purchase flower-shaped cookies and share with young women, or create a sunflower cookie by decorating a round sugar cookie with frosting in a tube. OPTION #2: Sunflower seeds. Tell young women that the sunny decisions we make each day determine our destiny. Each day we can plant in our mind and heart seeds of faith that will help us make those eternal decisions. Let's make those decisions early in life, so when temptations come we can say "no" to unrighteous choices. Then we can say "yes" to choices that will help our family be an eternal family.

MIDWEEK ACTIVITIES:
Choices & Consequence Trial Trail. Put the young women on trial as they learn which trail to follow that leads to the temple trail or the transgression trail.

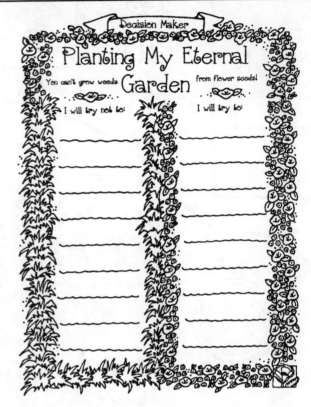

Planting My Eternal Garden

You can't grow weeds from flower seeds!

I will try not to: I will try to:

Step #1: Have someone talk about immodest dress, inappropriate music and movies (not just R, but also PG-13 rated), gossip, lack of prayer, cheating, etc., and what these can lead to.

Step #2: Set up and announce that you are having a trial of consequences leading to the right (temple trail) or left (trial trail), marking the floor.

Step #3: With the guidance of leaders, let young women take charge of listing choices and consequences on the board or poster.

Step #4: Divide young women into two groups. Have one group act out the right choices and consequences (going down the temple trail). Have the other act out the wrong choices and consequences (going down the trial trail). Then switch roles for each group so each group roleplays the right and wrong choices and consequences.

IDEAS: Notice as one persists in doing something that destroys the Spirit, she gets further and further away from the temple. List actions, e.g., inappropriate thoughts and desires could lead to immodest dress, which could lead to inappropriate actions, that in turn could lead to immorality, and possible pregnancy, single parenthood, family sadness, and heartache.

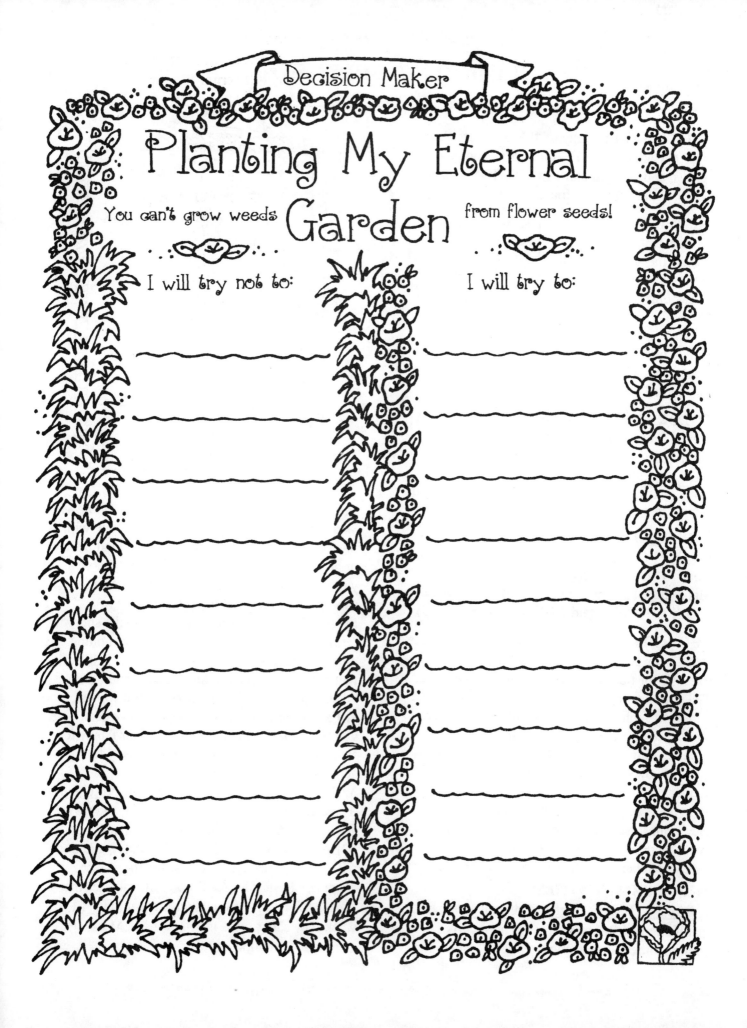

Decision Maker

Planting My Eternal Garden

You can't grow weeds   from flower seeds!

I will try not to: I will try to:

Lesson #9*   **FAMILY UNITY: I Will Create Family Ties**
(family unity checklist)

YOU'LL NEED: Copy of "I Will Create Family Ties" checklist (page 19) for each young woman, pencils, and colored markers. OPTION: Small pieces of flat rope or raffia.

ACTIVITY: Read Mosiah 18:8-9 and discuss the advantages of serving in their family. Ask young women to use this family unity checklist to list things they can do this coming week to create family unity (family ties). To decorate checklist, tie a piece of rope or raffia and glue it on checklist (if checklist was copied on cardstock paper).

Review quotations and Lesson Application (page 34) in Young Women Manual 3.*

COLOR SYMBOL: Color floral symbol on activity and scripture card. File activity in Young Women Value-able Journal behind the value tab.

Individual Worth (red rose)

PERSONAL PROGRESS* GOALS:
Beehive 1 (Divine Nature 6, Individual Worth 5, Good Works 5), Beehive 2 (Divine Nature 6, 7), Mia Maid 1 (Divine Nature 1, 3, 4, 5, Individual Worth 3, 7), Mia Maid 2 (Divine Nature 1, 7, 9)

THOUGHT TREAT: Licorice Rope. Purchase string licorice. Tie two pieces of licorice rope together, or tie a knot in the center of one piece. Tell young women that the more time they spend with their family, sharing thoughts and feelings, reading the scriptures, having family home evening, family prayer, and great meals together, the more they can create family ties. The memories they create will endure. This way everyone's family can be unified and strong. If they want to spend a lot of time with their friends, invite them to family activities and invite their family members to activities with their friends.

MIDWEEK ACTIVITIES:

1. Bite My Tongue Night. Tell young women that biting their tongue begins at home. Ask young women, Is this true or false? *"Sticks and*

stones will break my bones, but words will never hurt me." Give each young woman a twig with this saying printed on a tag attached. Find poetry or article about biting words that hurt. Serve a yummy dessert the girls can help make like a sundae, etc. Talk about the term *"bite your tongue,"* and what it means. Discuss the short-term and long-term consequences of not biting our tongues when we need to. Discuss situations that may come up with family and friends, and what you might say in place of hurtful words.

2. Family Fun Favorites Night. Have each young woman bring a member of their family to share and talk about their favorite family fun activities.

3. Family Fun Activity Card File or Notebook. Have young women bring their ideas, and review articles and books that give ideas on family fun. IDEAS: Seasonal party, sharing holiday traditions with family, creating food that fits the season. Have family start an ABC book of activities that starts with letters of the alphabet (e.g., On "M" week they can go to a movie, eat M&M candies and munch on popcorn).

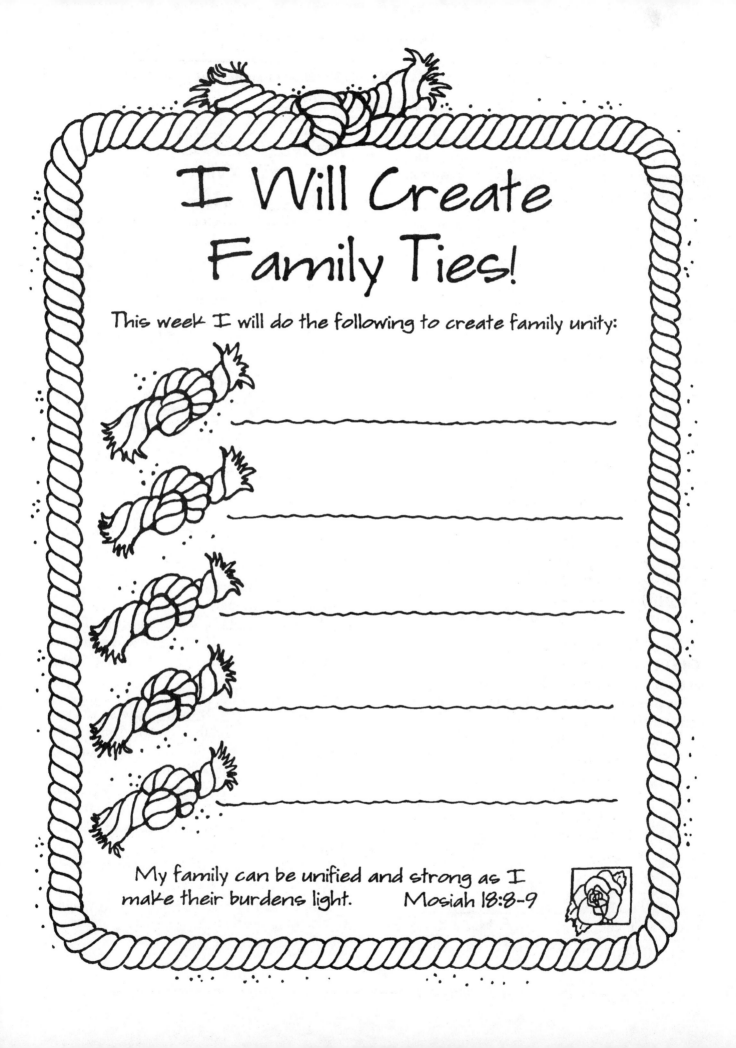

I Will Create Family Ties!

This week I will do the following to create family unity:

_____

_____

_____

_____

_____

My family can be unified and strong as I make their burdens light. Mosiah 18:8-9

Lesson #10*	**FAMILY ACTIVITIES: I Will Encourage Enjoyable Activities**
	(Family Fun Activity Sack)

YOU'LL NEED: Copy of sack label and activity wordstrips (pages 21-22), and an envelope or zip-close plastic sandwich bag for each young woman, pencils, and colored markers.

ACTIVITY: (1) Color and cut out the Family Fun Activity Sack label and wordstrips. (2) Glue label to an envelope or insert into a plastic bag. (3) Ask *Review Preparation #2 and Teacher preparation (page 35) in Young Women Manual 3*.*

young women to motivate their family to fun activities by drawing these activities out of the sack to do for family home evening. To review what's in the sack, have young women take turns drawing wordstrips from one sack. Read them aloud.

Encourage young women to invent their own ideas and place them on wordstrips to add to their Family Fun Activity Sack. (4) Review the 5 Ways to Create Memorable Moments on the label (detailed in the lesson*).

SUGGESTIONS: Ask young women to show and tell about activity books that they are using for family home evening. You'll find *Home-spun Fun Family Home Evenings* and *File Folder Family Home Evenings*, by Ross and Guymon-King available at LDS bookstores.

COLOR SYMBOL: Color floral symbol on scripture card. File activity in Young Women Value-able Journal behind the value tab.

Good Works (yellow sunflower)

PERSONAL PROGRESS* GOALS:
Beehive 1 (Good Works 6), Beehive 2 (Faith 2, Divine Nature 5, Good Works 4),
Mia Maid 1 (Faith 6, Individual Worth 2, 6, 8),
Mia Maid 2 (Divine Nature 4, Knowledge 1),
Laurel 1 & 2 Projects #1, 7, and 8 (page 79)

THOUGHT TREAT: Family T-Shirt Cookie. 1. Cut out sugar cookies in a T-shirt shape and decorate with frosting in different styles. If doing

for a midweek activity, use cookie paints (two drops of food coloring in 1 teaspoon of canned milk). Paint on cookies and bake. This is a fun activity young women can do in family home evening or for a family activity.

2. The family could also design matching T-shirts that read "I ❤ FHE" (Family Home Evening), or "I ❤ My Family," and wear it on Monday night.

MIDWEEK ACTIVITIES:

1. **Family Fun Sack Brainstorm.** Ask young women to write down their favorite family fun activities to share with the others. Type and photocopy their bright ideas to share.

2. **Family Activity Show-and-Tell.** Ask several young women to show others how to do their activity. They could bring games, have relay races, put on a play or skit, etc.

3. **Have Parents Share Ideas** on how to have a successful family home evening.

4. **Teach a Filing System** and encourage young women to file all their "worth keeping" ideas in files for easy retrieval.

PATTERN: Family Activities (sack label)

Fun Family Home Evening Activities to cut up and place in Family Fun Activity Sack:

- ♥ Family t-shirt making
- ☆ Greeting card making
- ♥ Family home evening planning, creating a FHE chart
- ☆ Scone making
- ♥ Checkers
- ☆ Award ribbon night
- ♥ Home hotel pretend
- ☆ Sack lunch supper
- ♥ Scripture relay
- ☆ Hum a hymn with actions
- ♥ Primary song sing-a-long
- ☆ Dress-up fashion show
- ♥ Milk shake sipping
- ☆ Balloon bouncing relays

- ☆ Shoe shining
- ♥ Alphabet activities
- ☆ Watch a movie with chairs lined up like a movie theater
- ♥ Put on a skit using stuffed toys
- ☆ Flannel board story creations
- ♥ Draw and guess (Pictionary game)
- ☆ Testimony meeting
- ♥ Secret pal week
- ☆ Room corner clean (divide and conquer)
- ♥ Ice cream parlor
- ☆ Un-birthday party
- ♥ Scripture search and share
- ☆ Testimony treasure hunt
- ♥ Pancake creations

☆ Love notes & jokes

♥ Ward library checkout

☆ Talent recital

♥ Brag bulletin board

☆ Surprise prize

♥ Gospel grab bag

☆ Puppet show

♥ Flashlight shadow dancing

☆ Design stationery

♥ Junk food shop and share

☆ Relay racing

♥ This is your life spotlight

☆ Scripture scavenger hunt

♥ Missionary motivators

☆ Testimony telegram

♥ Job General (assign and inspect)

♥ Hopscotch

☆ Temple grounds tour

♥ Mother May I

☆ Share Church magazine articles

♥ Gospel pictures show-and-tell

☆ Generation gap guess and tell

♥ Prophet guessing game

☆ Snap-a-bite-appetite food fun

♥ Play money shopping

☆ Choose the Right checkers

♥ Good deed secret service

☆ Choice and Consequence game

♥ Exercise sharing

☆ Photo fun

♥ Journal write'n'share

Lesson #11*	**FAMILY (Extended): I Will Be a Friend to Extended Family** *(closeness checklist and postcard)*

YOU'LL NEED: Copy of checklist and postcard (page 25) for each young woman, pencils, and colored markers.

ACTIVITY: Encourage young women to make time for extended family, to include them in

> *Review "We Can Strengthen These Relationships in Many Ways" Discussion (page 39), and Lesson Application (page 40) in Young Women Manual 3*.*

their circle of love, remembering that families are forever. If they begin now to develop strong family ties, they will not be alone when they are separated from their immediate family. They will have someone they can call or communicate with when they are in need, and someone they can serve. **STEPS TO BECOME CLOSE:** (1) Use the "I will be a friend to extended family," checklist to plan what you will do to become close to that chosen family member. (2) Circle or highlight several things you wish to do in the following year to become close to that person. Schedule these actions on a calendar this week. (3) Begin by sending this extended family member a postcard. Decorate the front, write a quick note, and send it off this week!

COLOR SYMBOL: Color floral symbol on activity and scripture card. File activity in Young Women Value-able Journal behind the value tab.

Good Works (yellow sunflower)

THOUGHT TREAT: Grammy Graham Cracker Award. Spotlight a grandmother in the ward. Interview family members to find stories of interest. Award her with a graham cracker with the words "Grammy Award" written in frosting. Present her with a bouquet of flowers or a small pant. Give each young woman a graham cracker and frosting in a tube to write the extended relative's name for which they wish to become close to (see activity above).

MIDWEEK ACTIVITIES:

1. Grammy Awards Night. Have young women create a potluck dinner for a grandmother or grandfather. Have them spotlight the grandparent and award them with a Grammy Award cookie or certificate or a Gramps Award cookie or certificate (for the grandfather).

2. "Relative"-ly Fun Night. Create a fun night for young women to bring one of their favorite relatives they are close to. Relatives can take turns sharing how they remember the young woman, spotlighting her for her kind deeds and warm ways.

3. Organize Family Greeting Cards. Create greeting card storage pockets for young women to store greeting cards months ahead to send to relatives. Young women can contact relatives to learn of their birthdays, and make homemade cards to send. CREATE POCKETS: Cut an 8 ½" x 11" sheet of paper in thirds. Glue the 1/3 piece of paper at the bottom of a whole 8 ½" x 11" sheet of paper on the sides and bottom. Write the month on each pocket, January - December, creating 12 pockets. Three-hole punch pockets to place in young women's journal. Glue a 3" x 5" card on the front of pockets to write special dates, e.g., holidays, birthdays, and their parents' anniversary. Don't forget thank you and get well cards.

4. Family Photo Session. Have young women bring some favorite family photos to show and tell about their extended family as they show photos. Ask them to tell one or two reasons why they love this extended family member, and share a fond experience or story about them. Remind them that as they expend their love to family members, they will create lasting memories they can share with their children.

 **Young Women Manual 3* and *Personal Progress* books are published by The Church of Jesus Christ of Latter-day Saints, Salt Lake City, Utah.

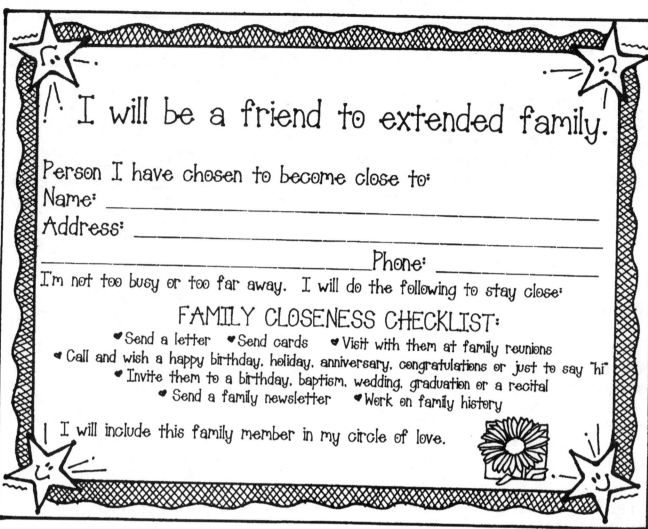

I will be a friend to extended family.

Person I have chosen to become close to:

Name: _____

Address: _____

_____ Phone: _____

I'm not too busy or too far away. I will do the following to stay close:

FAMILY CLOSENESS CHECKLIST:

♥ Send a letter ♥ Send cards ♥ Visit with them at family reunions
♥ Call and wish a happy birthday, holiday, anniversary, congratulations or just to say "hi"
♥ Invite them to a birthday, baptism, wedding, graduation or a recital
♥ Send a family newsletter ♥ Work on family history

I will include this family member in my circle of love.

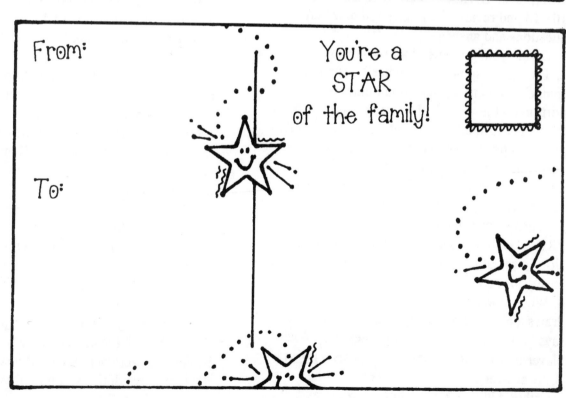

Decorate the front of the postcard, then write a quick note and send it off!

From:

To:

You're a
STAR
of the family!

Lesson #12*	**PRIESTHOOD BLESSINGS from Heavenly Father**
	(Priesthood Power Ponder game)

YOU'LL NEED: Copy of wheel (page 27) on colored cardstock paper, quiz cards and blessing wordstrips (pages 28-29), game instructions (below), a metal brad, and a zip-close plastic bag for each young woman, and colored markers.

> Review Teacher presentation (page 43),
> "Great Blessings Come ... through the
> Priesthood" (page 43) and priesthood circle
> poster (page 44) in Young Women Manual 3*.

ACTIVITY: Use this game as a lesson review.
1. Color and cut out wheel.
2. Mount part A on part B in the center with a metal brad (making the center hole loose to allow center piece to spin around).
3. Cut out priesthood quiz cards and blessing wordstrips and lay upside down on the table.
4. Young women can take the game home to use as a teaching tool during family home evening.

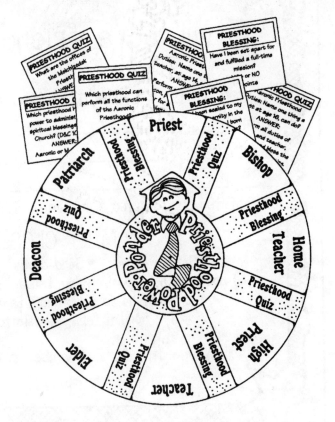

TO PLAY "PRIESTHOOD POWER PONDER" GAME: Start by reading D&C 107:18 and review the priesthood quiz card questions and answers.
1. Divide young women into two teams.
2. Take turns spinning the wheel. When the spinner points to a priesthood holder (the large portion on the wheel), the young woman who is taking her turn tells how that priesthood holder performs priesthood blessings, e.g., home teacher visits families each month to give a spiritual message and offer help where needed. Player then receives **5 points** for their team.
3. When spinner lands on the word PRIESTHOOD QUIZ, player draws and reads aloud a priesthood quiz card. The team can help answer, receiving **15 points** if correct.
4. When spinner lands on BLESSING, player draws a blessing wordstrip, reads it aloud, then says "yes" if they have had this blessing. When player tells about it, the team receives **5 points**. If the answer is "no," they have not yet had this priesthood blessing, the team still receives points.

PERSONAL PROGRESS* GOALS:
Beehive 1 (Individual Worth 3),
Mia Maid 1 (Good Works 1),
Mia Maid 2 (Individual Worth 1, 2)

THOUGHT TREAT: Priesthood Power Cupcakes. Display 15 frosted cupcakes in the center of the table with the letters PRIESTHOOD POWER written in frosting on top (one letter per cupcake). Remind young women that this power given to worthy men can bless our lives.

MIDWEEK ACTIVITIES:
1. **Priesthood Get to Know You Night.** Honor priesthood holders in your ward, talking about the various duties with a panel discussion, or play the game above.
2. **Priests Show Sacrament Preparation** room where they fill the cups and the prayer card behind the sacrament table. Priests can talk about the sacrament duties and how they feel about the priesthood they hold.

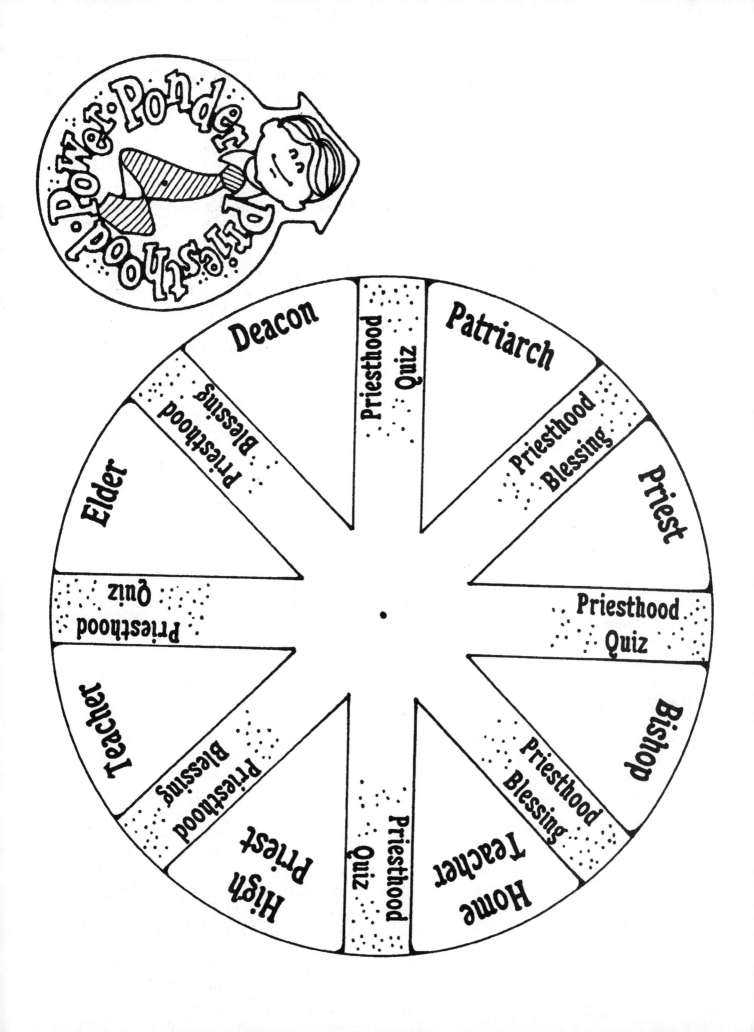

Power · Ponder · Priesthood · Power · Ponder · Priesthood

Deacon
Priesthood Quiz
Patriarch
Priesthood Blessing
Elder
Priest
Priesthood Quiz
Priesthood Quiz
Teacher
Bishop
Priesthood Blessing
Priesthood Blessing
High Priest
Home Teacher
Priesthood Quiz

PRIESTHOOD QUIZ
What are the offices of the Melchizedek Priesthood?
ANSWER: Elder
High Priest   Patriarch
Seventy   Apostle

PRIESTHOOD QUIZ
Which priesthood has the power to administer the spiritual blessings of the Church? (D&C 107:18)
ANSWER:
Aaronic or Melchizedek

PRIESTHOOD QUIZ
Which priesthood can baptize?

ANSWER:
Aaronic or Melchizedek

PRIESTHOOD QUIZ
Which priesthoods can bestow the gift of the Holy Ghost, Aaronic or Melchizedek?
ANSWER:
Melchizedek

PRIESTHOOD QUIZ
Which priesthood can ordain men to the office of the priesthood, Aaronic or Melchizedek?
ANSWER:
Melchizedek

PRIESTHOOD QUIZ
Which priesthood can perform sealing ordinances in the temple, Aaronic or Melchizedek?
ANSWER:
Melchizedek

PRIESTHOOD QUIZ
Which priesthood can perform all the functions of the Aaronic Priesthood?

ANSWER:
Melchizedek

PRIESTHOOD QUIZ
Aaronic Priesthood Duties: Name one thing a deacon, at age12, can do.
Answer:
Pass the sacrament, act as a messenger for priesthood leaders, collect fast offerings, care for Church buildings and grounds.

PRIESTHOOD QUIZ
Which priesthood can administer to the sick, Aaronic or Melchizedek?

ANSWER:
Melchizedek

PRIESTHOOD QUIZ
Aaronic Priesthood Duties: Name one thing a teacher, at age 14, can do.
ANSWER:
Perform all duties of a deacon, prepare bread and water for sacrament, can be assigned to be a home teacher.

PRIESTHOOD QUIZ
Aaronic Priesthood Duties: Name one thing a priest, at age 16, can do?
ANSWER:
Perform all duties of deacon and teacher, administer and bless the sacrament, and baptize.

PRIESTHOOD QUIZ
Aaronic Priesthood Duties: Name one thing an elder, at age 18, can do?
ANSWER:
Hold the Melchizedek Priesthood, serve a full-time mission, watch over the Church, give the gift of the Holy Ghost, conduct meetings, bless children, administer to the sick, and bless family members. Pass the sacrament, act as a messenger for priesthood leaders, collect fast offerings, care for Church buildings and grounds.

PATTERN: *PRIESTHOOD (Priesthood Power Ponder game)*

PRIESTHOOD BLESSING: Have I received baptism for the remissions of sins? YES or NO 5 points	**PRIESTHOOD BLESSING:** Have I been blessed when I was sick? YES or NO 5 points	**PRIESTHOOD BLESSING:** Have I received a patriarchal blessing? YES or NO 5 points
PRIESTHOOD BLESSING: Have I been confirmed after baptism to receive the gift of the Holy Ghost? YES or NO 5 points	**PRIESTHOOD BLESSING:** Have I had a chance to partake of the sacrament? YES or NO 5 points	**PRIESTHOOD BLESSING:** Have I been married in the temple? YES or NO 5 points
PRIESTHOOD BLESSING: Have I done temple ordinances for the dead? YES or NO 5 points	**PRIESTHOOD BLESSING:** Have I received all the temple ordinances? YES or NO 5 points	**PRIESTHOOD BLESSINGS:** Have I received a father's blessing? YES or NO 5 points
PRIESTHOOD BLESSING: Have I received a baby's name and a blessing? YES or NO 5 points	**PRIESTHOOD BLESSING:** Have I been set apart by the bishopric for a Church calling? YES or NO 5 points	**PRIESTHOOD BLESSING:** Have I been set apart for and fulfilled a full-time mission? YES or NO 5 points
PRIESTHOOD BLESSING: Have I received home teachers? YES or NO 5 points	**PRIESTHOOD BLESSING:** Have I had a personal interview with a member of the bishopric? YES or NO 5 points	**PRIESTHOOD BLESSING:** Have I been sealed to my family for eternity in the temple? Or was I born under the covenant? YES or NO 5 points

Lesson #13*

PRIESTHOOD Blesses Families
(Priesthood Power letter of appreciation stationery)

YOU'LL NEED: Copy of stationery (page 31) for each young woman, pencils or pens, and colored markers.

ACTIVITY: Using the stationery, encourage young women to write a letter of appreciation to her father or other priesthood leader. Express gratitude for priesthood leadership and blessings. Young women could write: "Dear Dad or Dear Bishop _____ . Thank you for being worthy to hold the priesthood of God. Thank you for honoring your priesthood. Your priesthood has blessed my life in the following ways..."
<u>Priesthood Holders to Write to</u>: Father, patriarch, General Authorities, stake president, bishop, home teachers, priesthood quorum leaders, friends who are worthy priesthood bearers).

Review Suggested Class Activity #1 in Young Women Manual 3*.

COLOR SYMBOL: Color floral symbol on scripture card.

Individual Worth (red rose)

THOUGHT TREAT: <u>Faith-ful Priesthood Cookie</u>. Purchase sandwich cookies or spread frosting between two graham crackers. Tell young women that one half of this cookie is the priesthood and the other half is our faith. The frosting in the middle represents the blessings we receive from the priesthood. With faith and the priesthood, we are able to receive the sweet blessings from the Lord.

MIDWEEK ACTIVITIES:
1. <u>Priesthood Leader Visit</u>. Take young women to visit with the stake president or bishop. Have him describe a typical week in the life of a stake president or bishop. Make a secret poster card ahead of time. Option: Glue candy bars on poster with thank-you notes from the young women. Have a question and answer time. Have the stake president or bishop express his feelings about his calling and how the young women can help. Present the poster card at the end.

2. <u>Temple Pre-view Interview</u>. Ask a member of the stake presidency or bishopric to talk to the young women about the questions asked in a temple recommend interview. Have him explain why the questions are asked and the importance of being ready at any time to enter the temple. Talk about the blessings of entering the temple.

3. <u>Patriarchal Blessings Pre-view</u>. Have a patriarch talk to the young women about receiving a patriarchal blessing and how they can prepare to receive this blessing.

4. <u>Father's Blessing Pre-view</u>. Ask a few fathers who have given father's blessings to come. Tell why a father's blessing is given and the types of blessings that are given to children who are worthy to receive a father's blessing.

5. <u>Dad and Daughter Night</u>. Invite the fathers to join their daughters in an evening of games, stories about fathers and daughters, and refreshments. Choose a theme and design activities around theme.

Lesson #14*

RESTORATION: Jesus Christ's Church Is Restored
(Apostasy Mirror teaching tool)

YOU'LL NEED: Copy of Apostasy Mirror and message (page 33) on colored paper for each young woman, scissors, and colored markers.

ACTIVITY: Create a teaching tool about the apostasy and restoration of the Church of Jesus Christ.

Review "There Was a Great Apostasy" Teacher presentation (page 49) in Young Women Manual 3.*

1. Color and cut out Apostasy Mirror and message.
2. Fold and glue back-to-back or stand up as a tent card.
3. Read the message and suggest young women enclose this in their scriptures or journal to use as a teaching tool to share with their family and friends.

COLOR SYMBOL: Color floral symbol on scripture card. File activity in Young Women Value-able Journal behind the value tab.

Good Works (yellow sunflower)

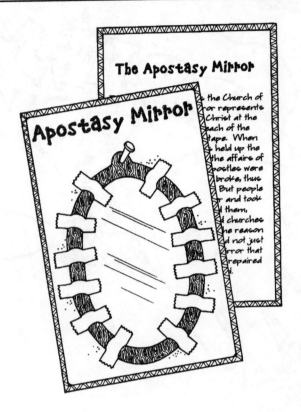

THOUGHT TREAT: Apostasy Cookie Crumble. Show a sandwich type cookie filled with frosting that you can take apart (e.g., Oreo cookie). Talk about the apostasy saying Option #1 or Option #2 as follows:

OPTION #1: Jesus organized the church of Jesus Christ when he was on the earth. After he and his 12 apostles died, the truth crumbled (separate cookie into two parts and crumble one cookie half). Christ's teachings crumbled away into many different beliefs. Then Joseph Smith prayed to find the true church. Because he asked Heavenly Father for the truth, The Church of Jesus Christ of Latter-day Saints was restored (take a good half of another cookie and place it on top of the frosting to make a complete sandwich cookie).

OPTION #2: The Bible is <u>one</u> testament of Jesus Christ (show one side of cookie), and the Book of Mormon is *another* testament of Jesus Christ (show other side of cookie). We can study the Bible and Book of Mormon and pray to know of the truth they hold. Our prayers help us gain a firm testimony that helps us keep the commandments, like the frosting that holds these two cookies together. As we search, ponder, and pray about these scriptures, we can gain a firm testimony that the church of Jesus Christ was restored in these latter days. Review the 8th Article of Faith.

MIDWEEK ACTIVITIES:

1. **Convert's Testimony Sharing.** Ask several converts to share their testimony of the restored gospel of Jesus Christ and answer questions.

2. **Signs of Apostasy Speaker.** Have a good speaker (seminary teacher, parent, Young Women leader, bishopric member) talk on the signs of apostasy and the dangers to avoid.

Apostasy Mirror

The Apostasy Mirror

This mirror represents the Church of Jesus Christ. The mirror represents the Church itself, with Christ at the top as the nail, and each of the apostles as a piece of tape. When Christ died, the apostles held up the mirror and took care of the affairs of the Church. When the apostles were killed, the mirror fell and broke, thus resulting in the apostasy. But people still saw good in the mirror and took pieces and built around them, resulting in the many varied churches of today. This exemplifies the reason we needed a restoration and not just a reformation...because a mirror that has been broken cannot be repaired -- it must be replaced.

Lesson #15*

ETERNAL LIFE: I Can Obtain the Celestial Kingdom
(Puzzled About Eternal Life? connected word find)

YOU'LL NEED: Copy Puzzled About Eternal Life? word find (page 35) for each young woman, pencils, and colored markers.

ACTIVITY:
Help young women review the five ways we can obtain the celestial kingdom

> *Review Chalkboard sample "To gain eternal life" (page 56) in Young Women Manual 3*.*

with this fun connected word find puzzle.
ANSWERS: (1) Keep the commandments, (2) Endure to the end, (3) Believe in Jesus Christ, (4) Be spiritually minded, (5) Be married in the temple.

COLOR SYMBOL: Color floral symbol on activity and scripture card. File activity in Young Women Value-able Journal behind the value tab.

Divine Nature (blue morning glory)

PERSONAL PROGRESS* GOALS:
Mia Maid 1 (Faith 3),
Mia Maid 2 (Divine Nature 6)

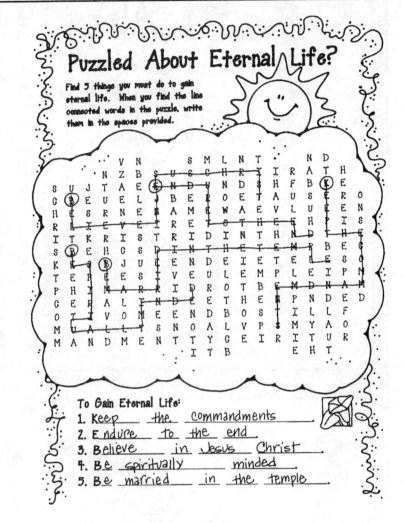

Puzzled About Eternal Life?

Find 5 things you must do to gain eternal life. When you find the line connected words in the puzzle, write them in the spaces provided.

To Gain Eternal Life:
1. Keep the commandments
2. Endure to the end
3. Believe in Jesus Christ
4. Be spiritually minded
5. Be married in the temple

THOUGHT TREAT: Eternal Life Rope. Tie licorice rope pieces together into five knots/ties, making a ring. Place the ring around young women's necks and point to the five knots, talking about the five ways we can prepare to gain eternal life (shown above). Tell young women that eternal life is tied directly to the gospel of Jesus Christ. If we follow these guidelines we can create family ties that last forever.

MIDWEEK ACTIVITIES:
1. House of Israel Discussion. Have a patriarch come and explain the House of Israel and the blessings associated with it, using maps, etc.

2. Nephi's Emotional Plea. Read and discuss carefully 2 Nephi 3.

3. Eternal Life Night. Divide young women into five groups. Ask each group to design a booth to represent one of the five ways we can gain eternal life: (1) Keep the commandments, (2) Endure to the end, (3) Believe in Jesus Christ, (4) Be spiritually minded, and (5) Be married in the temple. Give them some time on Sunday during class to discuss the design of their booth. That night, as a group, ask each booth committee to present their ideas.
IDEAS:
1. Copy articles from the Church magazines.
2. Create favors to give away, post pictures (found in the ward library).
3. Have speaker or young woman give a 2 ½ minute talk.

Puzzled About Eternal Life?

Find 5 things you must do to gain eternal life. When you find the line connected words in the puzzle, write them in the spaces provided.

```
          V  N          S  M  L  N  T        N  D
       N  Z  B  S  U  S  G  H  R  I  I  R  A  T  H
S  U  J  T  A  E  E  N  D  U  R  O  E  T  H  F  B  K  E      H
C  B  E  U  E  L  J  B  E  R  O  E  A  V  A  U  U  E  P      E     O
H  E  U  R  N  E  N  A  M  E  W  A  T  H  E  L  H  P  T      R     N
R  L  K  E  E  I  A  R  E  T  A  T  H  E  N  E  D  B  B      E     S
I  T  E  R  I  R  S  R  I  D  T  I  E  E  M  N  P  E  I      I     E
S  B  E  H  G  S  D  I  N  H  H  E  E  T  E  M  L  E  N      H     C
K  E  P  B  J  U  E  E  N  D  E  I  I  T  L  E  E  N  D      E     O
T  P  E  E  E  S  I  V  U  E  L  O  T  P  I  L  I  D  L      S     M
P  H  I  M  A  R  R  I  D  R  O  T  E  B  N  L  N  L  A      P     M
G  E  R  A  L  I  N  D  E  E  T  H  H  E  E  M  D  Y  U      A     D
O  T  I  V  O  M  E  N  D  E  H  O  B  N  P  P  L  I  T      F     F
M  U  A  L  L  Y  S  N  O  A  O  S  L  T  S  I  Y  T  H      O     O
M  A  N  D  M  E  N  T        T  B  G  E  V  R  M  U            R
                    I  T           C     I  P  E  T
```

To Gain Eternal Life:
1. K_____ _____
2. E_____ _____ _____.
3. B_____ _____.
4. B____ _____.
5. B____ _____.

Lesson #16*   **TEMPLE ENDOWMENT: I Will Prepare for Eternal Life**
(Ladder to Eternal Life word find)

YOU'LL NEED: Copy word find (page 48) for each young woman, pencils, and colored markers.

ACTIVITY: Read D&C 124:40-41 with young women, and help then climb the ladder to eternal

Review Chalkboard illustration (page 58) in Young Women Manual 3.*

life with this challenging word search. First highlight (or color the word) "temple endowment" on the ladder and on the word maze.

To Do Word Search:
1. Find the words on the ladder on the left in the word maze on the right.
2. Circle the matching words in the word maze.
3. Remember, each step you take on the Eternal Life Ladder will help you feel that much closer to our Heavenly Father and Jesus.

COLOR SYMBOL: Color floral symbol on activity and scripture card. File activity in Young Women Value-able Journal behind the value tab.

Choice & Accountability (orange poppy)

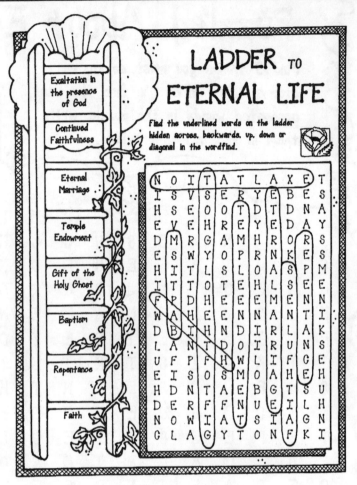

LADDER TO ETERNAL LIFE

Find the underlined words on the ladder hidden across, backwards, up, down or diagonal in the wordfind.

Exaltation in the presence of God
Continued Faithfulness
Eternal Marriage
Temple Endowment
Gift of the Holy Ghost
Baptism
Repentance
Faith

THOUGHT TREAT: Ladder Lunch.
1. Pack a simple lunch for each young woman, with a half sandwich, some chips, and a cookie.
2. OPTION: Photocopy (reducing the Eternal Life Ladder 70% and glue it on the lunch sack.
3. As you eat the lunch, talk about the eight steps to take and how you can stay on the straight and narrow path:
Step #1: Faith (in Jesus Christ)
Step #2: Repentance
Step #3: Baptism
Step #4: Gift of the Holy Ghost
Step #5: Temple Endowment
Step #5: Eternal Marriage
Step #6: Continued Faithfulness
Step #7: Exaltation in the presence of God

MIDWEEK ACTIVITIES:
1. **Bishop Talk.** Have the bishop talk about the temple and go over the temple interview questions. Perhaps have each young woman obtain a temple recommend for baptism for the dead only. Have the young women set a goal to renew that recommend annually until and beyond the time comes for their personal endowment. If possible, each year, all young women could go together to do baptisms for the dead.
2. **Temple Dress Fashion Show.** Arrange with a local bridal shop to show some dresses; perhaps the young women could model them. Be sure to stress modesty for the temple and reception.

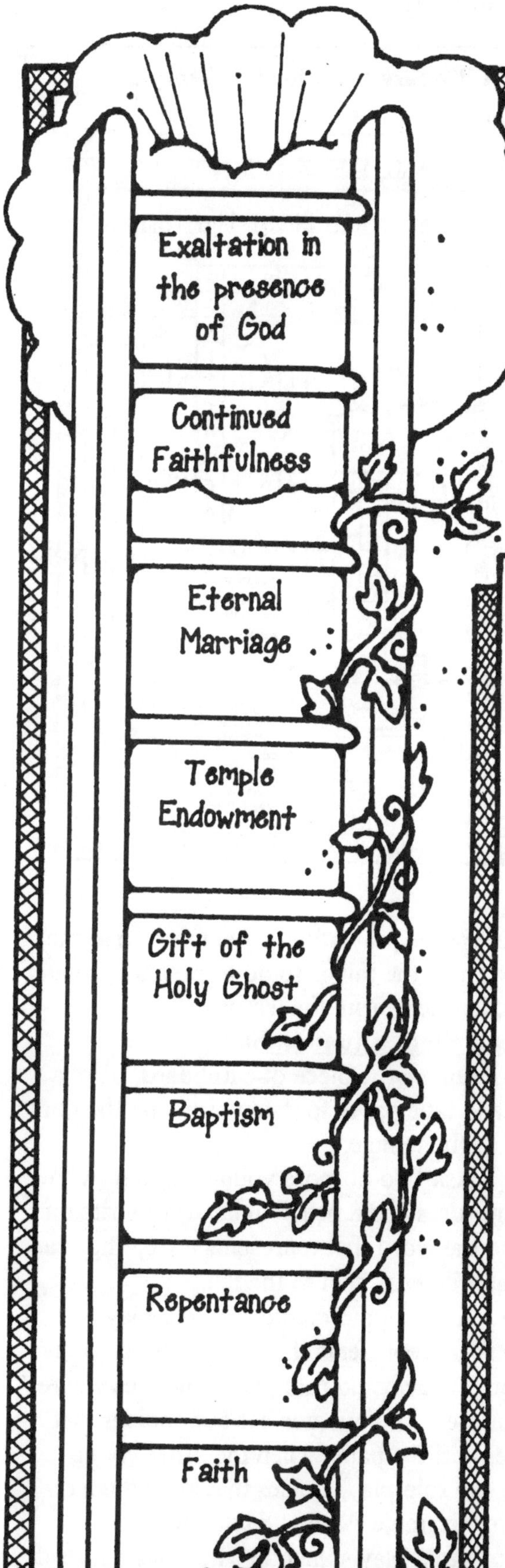
Exaltation in the presence of God
Continued Faithfulness
Eternal Marriage
Temple Endowment
Gift of the Holy Ghost
Baptism
Repentance
Faith

LADDER TO ETERNAL LIFE

Find the underlined words on the ladder hidden across, backwards, up, down or diagonal in the wordfind.

N	O	I	T	A	T	L	A	X	E	T
I	S	V	S	E	R	Y	E	B	E	S
H	S	E	O	O	T	D	T	D	N	A
E	V	E	H	R	E	Y	E	D	A	Y
D	M	R	G	A	M	H	R	O	R	S
E	S	W	Y	O	P	R	N	K	E	S
H	I	T	L	S	L	O	A	S	P	M
I	T	T	O	T	E	H	L	S	E	E
F	P	D	H	E	E	E	M	E	N	N
W	A	H	E	E	N	N	A	N	T	I
D	B	I	H	N	D	I	R	L	A	K
L	A	N	T	D	O	I	R	U	N	S
U	F	P	F	H	W	L	I	F	C	E
E	I	S	O	S	M	O	A	H	E	H
H	D	N	T	A	E	B	G	T	S	U
D	E	R	F	F	N	U	E	I	L	H
N	O	W	I	A	T	S	I	A	G	N
C	L	A	G	Y	T	O	N	F	K	I

| *Lesson #17** | **TEMPLE PREPARATION:** I Will Prepare to Enter the Temple *(temple scripture clue puzzle)* |

YOU'LL NEED: Copy temple scripture clue puzzle (page 39) for each young woman, pencils, and colored markers.

ACTIVITY: Help young women complete this scripture clue puzzle, to learn ways they can prepare to enter the temple. Search the scriptures to find clues to the missing words and write them in the squares.

Review Discussion ideas #1-3 (page 60) in Young Women Manual 3.*

COLOR SYMBOL: Color floral symbol on activity and scripture card. File activity in Young Women Value-able Journal behind the value tab.

Divine Nature (blue morning glory)

PERSONAL PROGRESS* GOALS:
Beehive 1 (Individual Worth 6),
Beehive 2 (Divine Nature 2, Choice & Accountability 5)

THOUGHT TREAT: Temple Mints. Give each young woman a temple-shaped mint, six small butter mints, or Starlite mints. Tell them that Heavenly Father and Jesus "mint" for them to enter the temple, and partake of the covenants there that will prepare them for the celestial kingdom. Read D&C 124:40-41 *("I may reveal mine ordinances")* and D&C 14:7 *("keep my commandments, endure to the end . . . have eternal life")*.

MIDWEEK ACTIVITIES:
1. "IF IT IS TO BE, IT IS UP TO ME" Night.
Have one or two speakers who have been through the temple come. Have them express that before they went to the temple, their desire to go to the temple was foremost in their mind. Tell how their path had distractions and how they were led in different directions. Tell how through consistent right choices, they were able to go to the temple. These are tender experiences and could be faith promoting. Obtain the bishop's

approval and be prayerful. Re-emphasize to the young women the things to do to prepare to enter the temple (ideas from the lesson).
2. Temple Steps Situation Skits.
Step #1: On a large piece of cardboard, paint a temple and tape paper footstep prints on the floor leading to the temple.
Step #2: Ask two or more young women (with their scriptures and a pencil in hand) to write on footprint the word that represents a step they can take that will lead them to the temple.
Step #3: Ask them to create and role-play a situation that represents the word written on the footprint. They could role-play opposites where one or more young women act out choices that take them off the path. Then the other young women can role-play choices that keep them on the path. Example: Write "Faith" on the footstep. Role-play someone who does not read the scriptures, who watches television instead. Role-play a young woman who reads the scriptures (see 2 Nephi 31:10).

I Will Prepare to Enter the Temple

Find the missing word by reading the scripture and then find its location in the puzzle.

- Be faithful in the testimony of _____ Christ. (D&C 138: 12)

- Live the law of _____. (Jacob 2:28)

- Keep the _____. (Alma 7:16)

- Choose a worthy companion to _____. (D&C 132: 19-20)

- Talk to those who have been through the _____. (Alma 34:36)

- Gain a _____ of the Savior. (Alma 6:8)

- Search the _____. (3 Nephi 10:14)

*Lesson #18**	**TEMPLE MARRIAGE:** My Family Can Be Together Forever	
	(Sacred Triangle mobile)	

YOU'LL NEED: Copy of triangle (page 41) for each young woman on colored cardstock paper, and of Mr. and Mrs. Promises treat label (page 42) and a small bag of M&M candies for each young woman, glue or tape, pencils, paper punch, string, and colored markers.

> *Review Object lesson and Conclusion (page 65) in Young Women Manual 3*.*

ACTIVITY: Create a sacred triangle mobile to remind young women of the sacred triangle of eternal marriage (God, husband, and wife).

1. Color and cut out triangle.

2. Help young women make the promise by memorizing the promise on the triangle.

3. Remind young women that marriage is a sacred promise, and Heavenly Father and Jesus (God) want us to be married in the temple, sealed to our husband and children forever. Families can be together forever with Heavenly Father's plan of temple marriage.

3. Write things they will do to prepare to enter the temple and live a righteous life:

♥ Keep the commandments

♥ Read the scriptures

♥ Learn about Jesus Christ

♥ Be chaste

♥ Choose a worthy companion.

4. Paper punch holes in the top of triangle. Have young women hang triangle in their room as a reminder.

COLOR SYMBOL: Color floral symbol on activity and scripture card. File activity in Young Women Value-able Journal behind the value tab.

Divine Nature (blue morning glory)

PERSONAL PROGRESS* GOALS:
Mia Maid 1 (Divine Nature 8),
Mia Maid 2 (Divine Nature 2)

THOUGHT TREAT: M&M Mr. and Mrs. Candies. Give each young woman a small

package of M&M candies with a label glued on bag. Copy Mr. and Mrs. Promises label (see pattern on page 42). Color, cut out, fold, and staple label (on sides). Insert M&M candies at the top the bag shown below.

MIDWEEK ACTIVITIES:

1. Companion Common Goal Discussion. Discuss the blessings of common goals in a marriage companion.
Discuss the dangers of dating nonmembers in hopes of converting them. Find prophets' quotes. Express the supreme importance of temple marriage.

2. M&M Marvelous Marriage Discussion.
Talk about Mr. and Mrs. Marvelous marriages. Tell about the prophet and his wife. Have someone who has a temple marriage come as a couple to discuss temple marriage. As you eat M&M candies, list on the board what makes a marvelous marriage.

Things I will
do to prepare:

Wife

My Promise:

I will prepare
now to be
worthy of
participating
in the sacred
triangle of
eternal
marriage.

God

Husband

glue

PATTERN: Temple Marriage (M&M candies label)

Mr. and Mrs. Promises

MR. AND MRS. PROMISES: M&M stands for Mr. and Mrs. Eat three M&M candies at a time and remember the three point triangle that represents God, husband and wife. Each time you date, remember your promise: "I will prepare now to be worthy of participating in the sacred triangle of eternal marriage." Every choice you make can lead you closer to the temple.

*Lesson #19**	**HERITAGE:** I Will Pass on Righteous Traditions
	(My Conversion to the Gospel journal)

YOU'LL NEED: Copy several journal pages (page 44) for each young woman, pencils, and colored markers.

ACTIVITY: Tell young women they can leave a legacy of love to their families in word and deed.

Review Writing activity (page 68) in Young Women Manual 3.*

Begin by writing your testimony about your conversion to the gospel of Jesus Christ. With this, future generations can read of your love for the Lord and the gospel. How you feel now about the gospel can be of great worth and value to your family now and to your posterity (future generations).

THINGS YOU COULD WRITE ABOUT:
❤Spiritual feelings about the scriptures, our Savior, church leaders, family members, or friends who have strengthened your testimony ❤Paying tithing ❤Attending church ❤Obeying specific commandments ❤Faith ❤Your baptism ❤Receiving the Holy Ghost ❤The priesthood ❤ Missionary work ❤Young women testimonies ❤Examples to follow ❤Scripture heroes ❤Experiences of being baptized for the dead ❤Desire to be married in the temple ❤Desire to live a Christlike life ❤Desire to serve others ❤The joy that comes through service ❤Parents, brothers and sisters, and relatives who have influenced you ❤Living specific gospel principles ❤Ways the Holy Ghost has witnessed to you that the gospel and the scriptures are true ❤Your testimony

COLOR SYMBOL: Color floral symbol on activity and scripture card. File activity in Young Women Value-able Journal behind the value tab.

Individual Worth (red rose)

PERSONAL PROGRESS* GOALS:
Beehive 1 (Individual Worth 1),
Beehive 2 (Individual Worth 2, 5),
Mia Maid 2 (Individual Worth 4-8)

THOUGHT TREAT: Legacy of Love Journal Cake. Bake a square or 9" x 12" cake, frost and decorate like a journal page with the words "Legacy of Love" at the top with a heart symbol. Tell young women that they can leave a legacy of love with their children and posterity through the many generations of time. Ask young women to write about their conversion to the gospel and testify of their desire to live it. This way their influence can be widespread, like dropping a pebble in a pool of water, rippling out from generation to generation. Even when they are no longer here to share their testimony, their written testimony will stand as a witness that they know the gospel of Jesus Christ is true. This will be one of their most treasured possessions.

MIDWEEK ACTIVITY:
Traditional Treasures. Ask each young woman to share a righteous family tradition. Write down ideas to copy and share. Title it, "Traditional Treasures."

My Conversion to the Gospel

Lesson #20*	**MISSIONARY WORK:** I Will Support Missionary Work
	(Missionary Support crossword puzzle)

YOU'LL NEED: Copy Missionary Support crossword puzzle (page 46) for each young woman, pencils, and colored markers.

ACTIVITY:

Review Question and chalkboard discussion (page 74) in Young Women Manual 3.

Remind young women what they can do to help missionaries meet their responsibilities in their work for the Lord. Young women can read clues and fill in the missing words. Read activity for details.

ANSWERS: (1) introduce, (2) time, (3) serve, (4) continue, (5) help, (6) watch, (7) television, (8) rules, (9) respect, (10) write, (11) talk, (12) phone.

GROUP ACTIVITY: <u>Missionary Support List Review</u>. This can be done after young women have filled in the missing words.

1. Ahead of time write in the missing words and photocopy (enlarge) the Missionary Support List.

2. Cut up sentences into sentence or groups of words wordstrips, and place them face up in front of the young women.

3. Divide young women into two teams across from each other in a circle with wordstrips in the center.

4. Tell young women that at the word "go," to find the wordstrips to complete as many sentences as they can. CAUTION: Ask young women not to pick up the wordstrips until they are sure they have a complete sentence. This way both teams can see the words.

5. Ask young women to announce when they have made a match by saying reverently, "Missionary Support." A completed sentence wins a point for their team. The team with the most points wins!

6. To review, ask each young woman team to read their Missionary Support sentences aloud.

COLOR SYMBOL: Color floral symbol on activity and scripture card. File activity in Young Women Value-able Journal behind the value tab.

Good Works (yellow sunflower)

PERSONAL PROGRESS* GOALS:
<u>Beehive 1</u> (Faith 3, 5, 7, 8), <u>Beehive 2</u> (Faith 5, 6), <u>Mia Maid 1</u> (Faith 2, 5), <u>Mia Maid 2</u> (Faith 2, 8), <u>Laurel 1 & 2</u> Project #5 (page 79)

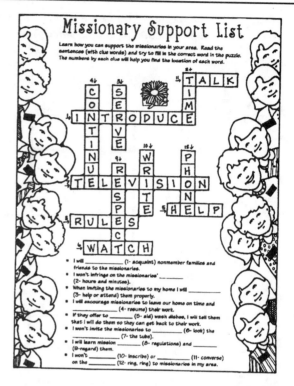

THOUGHT TREAT: <u>Missionary Tracting Treats</u>. Share with young women a trail mix with cereal, dried fruit, and nuts. As they eat, ask them to imagine what missionary tracting is like and share their thoughts with the others.

MIDWEEK ACTIVITY: <u>Missionary "We Care" Package</u>. (1) Send a large card or paper with all the young women's encouraging words and good news to each missionary in the ward. This could be done as an assembly line with projects laid out on the table for each missionary. (2) Put together a care package with new toothbrush, gum, candy, handkerchief, tie (can buy used or ask priesthood leaders to donate). (3) Take a photo of young women saying, "Hi, Elder _____," holding a sign, etc. Brainstorm on what to send and say. Obtain the bishop's approval of what you are sending. Write on the package: "<u>'We Care' Package</u>." (4) If including a tape, ask young women to find a poem, quote, or scripture they can read after they say, "Hi, my name is _____." Tell the missionary's parents you are sending a package (in case they have something to enclose).

Missionary Support List

Learn how you can support the missionaries in your area. Read the sentences (with clue words) and try to fill in the correct word in the puzzle. The numbers by each clue will help you find the location of each word.

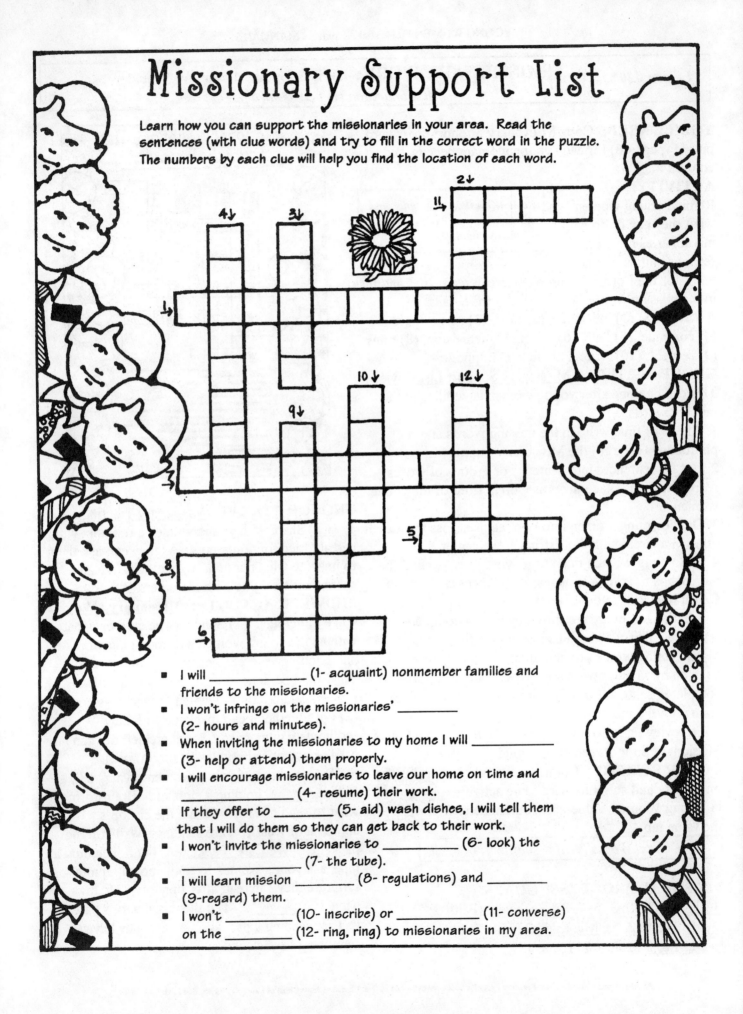

- I will _____ (1- acquaint) nonmember families and friends to the missionaries.
- I won't infringe on the missionaries' _____ (2- hours and minutes).
- When inviting the missionaries to my home I will _____ (3- help or attend) them properly.
- I will encourage missionaries to leave our home on time and _____ (4- resume) their work.
- If they offer to _____ (5- aid) wash dishes, I will tell them that I will do them so they can get back to their work.
- I won't invite the missionaries to _____ (6- look) the _____ (7- the tube).
- I will learn mission _____ (8- regulations) and _____ (9-regard) them.
- I won't _____ (10- inscribe) or _____ (11- converse) on the _____ (12- ring, ring) to missionaries in my area.

Lesson #21*   **MISSIONARY SERVICE:**   Follow the Prophets and Share the Gospel
(GUESS WHO? Prophets cross match)

YOU'LL NEED: Copy of cross match (page 48) for each young woman, pencils, and markers.

ACTIVITY: Remind young women of some of the prophets through the ages who shared the gospel of Jesus Christ with others.

> *Review Chalkboard discussion (page 76) in Young Women Manual 3*.*

With this Guess Who? Prophets cross match, young women can read the scriptures and imagine what it would be like to be a prophet, who was sometimes the only one preaching the gospel. From this activity young women can learn ways they can prepare themselves to share the gospel with others.

Guess Who? Prophets Cross Match:
1. Read the description and guess who the prophet is and the missing words.
2. Read the scriptures by the prophet's name to make sure you are right.
3. Write in the prophet's name and the missing words.
4. Draw a line from the description to the prophet.

COLOR SYMBOL: Color floral symbol on activity and scripture card. File activity in Young Women Value-able Journal behind the value tab.

> *Good Works (yellow sunflower)*

PERSONAL PROGRESS* GOALS:
Beehive 2 (Faith 3, 4, Good Works 7, Integrity 4),
Mia Maid 1 (Knowledge 2, Good Works 6),
Mia Maid 2 (Faith 4, 6, 9)

THOUGHT TREAT: Smooth Sailing Fellow-"ship" Sandwich. Make a half sandwich for the boat and place a toothpick in a slice of processed cheese for the sail. Tell young women to have courage as they sail into friend-ships with those who are not members of our faith. Think of where you would be today without the gospel

and where others might be tomorrow if they had the gospel.

MIDWEEK ACTIVITIES:
1. **Follow the Suggested Activities #1-5** (page 77) in Young Women's manual 3*.
2. **Canoe Chats.** Go on an imaginary or real ride (on blankets or water) with someone you would like to get to know better, Laurel with a Beehive or Mia Maid with a Beehive. When you return, report one thing that impressed you about your partner. Talk about getting to know another person before you begin this activity, what to say, how to develop a friendship, and how to help another person feel comfortable. After young women have shared their comments about the canoe trip, talk about how they might fellowship a nonmember.

GUESS WHO Shared the Gospel?

Prophets cross match

Daniel -
Daniel 6:16, 22-23

Moses - Moses 1:26,
Exodus 12:40

Nephi - 1 Nephi 3:7

Noah -
Moses 8:19-20, 30

Enos - Enos 1:13

Lehi - 1 Nephi 1:16

Alma - Alma 8:10

Abinadi
- Mosiah 11:20-21

❤The Prophet _____ wrestled in mighty _____ that God would pour out his _____ upon the people that he might baptize them unto repentance.

❤The Prophet _____ wrote about the many things he has saw in _____ and _____.

❤The Prophet _____ told the people to _____ and _____ to God, or they would be delivered into the hands of their _____.

❤The Prophet _____ called upon the children of men to _____, but they harkened _____ unto his words, and were _____ed.

❤The Prophet _____ was cast into a _____ of _____ because he refused to sin. Because he _____ in his God, an _____ was sent to shut the _____ _____.

❤The Prophet _____ said the Lord gives ___ ___ commandments unto the children of men, save he shall _____ a way that they may accomplish what he commanded.

❤The Prophet _____ was commanded to _____ the people of _____ from _____ of _____ years.

❤The Prophet _____ wanted to preserve a _____ of the _____ that it might be brought to the _____ to bring them unto salvation.

Lesson #22*	**ETERNAL PERSPECTIVE:** I Can Face Trials
	(What I Want to "Bee" Eternally mirror motivators)

YOU'LL NEED: Copy of mirror motivators (page 50) on colored cardstock paper for each young woman, and colored markers.

ACTIVITY: Create these mirror motivators that young women can tape to their mirror to remind them of the woman

Review Suggested Activities (page 83) in Young Women Manual 3.*

they can become by: reading the scriptures to gain a testimony of truth, learning about the Savior's mission and atonement, preparing to receive a patriarchal blessing, and overcoming weaknesses such as procrastination and anger.
1. Color and cut out cards.
2. Ask young women to write on the back of each card how they can achieve this goal, and how achieving this goal will help them eternally as they face trials in mortal life.
3. Ask them to picture in their minds the woman they will become if they do what is on the card. Ask them to mentally contemplate who they will be if they do not do what is on the card.

COLOR SYMBOL: Color floral symbol on activity and scripture card. File activity in Young Women Value-able Journal behind the value tab.

Knowledge (green ivy)

PERSONAL PROGRESS* GOALS:
Mia Maid 1 (Faith 6),
Mia Maid 2 (Knowledge 2, 3)

THOUGHT TREAT:
Sweet Eternity Honey Taffy.
1. Give each young woman a bag of honey taffy.
2. See "Buzz to Heaven" tag (page 58)
3. Tell young women that bees work very

hard to produce honey, and we can work hard now to become the woman we want to be eternally.

MIDWEEK ACTIVITIES:
1. **Trial Talk.** Have someone come and talk about how they faced their trials, e.g. physical handicap, the death of a loved one, etc. Let them tell their story and answer questions. You could also have someone come who has been in the war and seen suffering and devastation. You might even invite someone from another country to come and talk about the trials they have faced. Talk about solutions to specific trials.
2. **Wheel Chair Walk.** Go to a nursing home or care center and take someone in a wheel chair for a walk, and/or visit to cheer and brighten their world.

I want to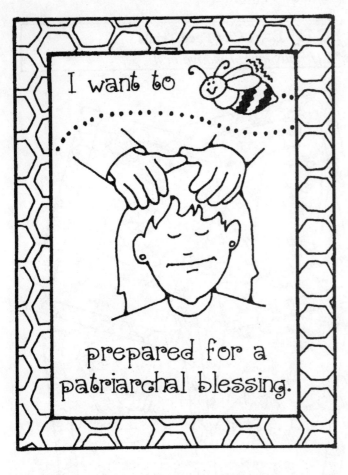
prepared for a
patriarchal blessing.

I want to
more like Jesus
as I follow in
his steps.

I want to
righteous by reading
the scriptures daily.

I want to
of service
to others.

Lesson #23*	**OPPOSITION Can Make Me Strong** *(Turn Trials into Triumphs match game)*

YOU'LL NEED: Copy one set of Triumph and Trial match cards and rules (pages 52-54) on colored cardstock paper, a zip-close plastic bag for each young woman, scissors, and markers.

ACTIVITY: Remind young women of the 12 ways we can overcome sorrow, disappointment, and depression with this

> *Review Chalkboard discussion (page 85) in Young Women Manual 3*.*

Turn Trials into Triumphs match game.
(1) Color and cut out cards, and game rules.
(2) Place game rules and cards in zip-close bag.
(3) Follow rules to play game.

TURN TRIALS INTO TRIUMPHS:
President Ezra Taft Benson told of 12 ways we can overcome sorrow, disappointment, and depression (*Ensign*, Nov. 1974, pp. 65-67). These 12 ways are represented on the Triumph cards #1-12 (on page 54 and listed below). After playing the game, ask young women to write ideas on the back of their cards, and ponder them during the week. <u>12 Ways to Overcome Sorrow, Disappointment, and Depression</u>: (1) Repentance, (2) Prayer, (3) Service, (4) Work, (5) Health, (6) Reading, (7) Blessing, (8) Fasting, (9) Friends, (10) Music, (11) Endurance, (12) Goals.

COLOR SYMBOL: Color floral symbol on scripture card. File activity in Young Women Value-able Journal behind the value tab.

Integrity (purple pansy)

PERSONAL PROGRESS* GOALS:
<u>Beehive 1</u> (Integrity 2), Beehive 2 (Divine Nature 4, Choice & Accountability 8), <u>Mia Maid 1</u> (Knowledge 7)

THOUGHT TREAT: <u>Opposition Eggs</u>. Color a dozen eggs and draw a face, picture, or symbol on each egg to represent the 12 ways we can overcome sorrow, disappointment, and

depression. Name the 12 ways, give each young woman an egg with this "Egg"-stra Strength note attached (shown above).

> **"EGG"- STRA STRENGTH NEEDED:**
> If you try "egg"-stra hard each day to overcome trials, you will obtain the "egg"-stra strength to overcome the next trial. This way you can obtain the "egg"-stra blessings that are in store for you eternally.

MIDWEEK ACTIVITIES:
1. <u>Opposition Comedies</u>. Create situation comedies and give the script to young women. Break up into groups and come up with a skit to share. Show solutions, e.g., "Malorie accepted a date with Patrick and then Prince Charming asked her out on the same night," etc.
2. <u>Opposite Night</u>. Young women teach young men how to sew on a button, quilt, or bake a dessert like a pie, etc. Then young men show young women how to change a tire, repair a leaky faucet, etc.
3. <u>Opposites Attract, and Like Attracts Like</u>. Talk about married couples who are opposite from each other in skills and likes and dislikes. Say, "Opposites often attract, as when a person has a quality that the other person doesn't have, but it is a quality he or she admires." Then talk about how "like attracts like." Having the same values in the gospel can hold an eternal marriage together.

Trials and Triumphs
Match Game Rules

1. Mix up and turn all the cards face down.
2. Divide into two teams.
3. Each team takes a turn trying to make a match. (Matching cards will have the same number.)
4. When a match is made, read both cards aloud.
5. Talk about the trial and tell others what they can do to turn it into a triumph.
6. Each team gets a point for every match they make. The team with the most points wins.

Trials and Triumphs
Match Game Rules

1. Mix up and turn all the cards face down.
2. Divide into two teams.
3. Each team takes a turn trying to make a match. (Matching cards will have the same number.)
4. When a match is made, read both cards aloud.
5. Talk about the trial and tell others what they can do to turn it into a triumph.
6. Each team gets a point for every match they make. The team with the most points wins.

Trial	Trial	Trial
1. I felt guilty about a lie I told.	2. I felt lost and didn't know what to do.	3. I felt gloomy because nobody did anything for me!
Trial	Trial	Trial
4. I felt lazy and wanted to goof around.	5. I felt sick and depressed after sitting all day.	6. I felt angry and frustrated after reading something I shouldn't have.
Trial	Trial	Trial
7. I felt very confused about a problem but didn't ask for a blessing.	8. I felt saddened about an experience and needed my spirit to be strengthened.	9. I felt lonely.
Trial	Trial	Trial
10. I felt agitated and contentious after hearing a popular album.	11. I felt like I wanted to give up trying.	12. I felt like I would never accomplish anything.

Triumph

1. I felt peace after repenting.

Triumph

2. I felt my Heavenly Father's love when I prayed.

Triumph

3. I forgot about my problem when I served my neighbor.

Triumph

4. I felt a great sense of accomplishment when my work was done!

Triumph

5. I felt strong and happy after my exercises.

Triumph

6. I felt enlightened after reading a good book.

Triumph

7. I felt comforted after a father's blessing.

Triumph

8. I felt a spiritual strength even though I was fasting.

Triumph

9. I felt uplifted when I was with good friends.

Triumph

10. I felt soothed and relaxed after listening to good music.

Triumph

11. I felt the Spirit when I decided to keep going.

Triumph

12. I felt excited when I reached a difficult goal.

Lesson #24*

AGENCY: I Will Follow Jesus Christ
(Agency Actions scripture challenge)

YOU'LL NEED: Copy of scripture challenge (page 56) for each young woman, pencils, and colored markers.

ACTIVITY: Read D&C 58:28 to help young women know that they are agents unto themselves to choose evil or good.

Review Chalkboard discussion (page 89 and Suggested Activity #1 (page 90) in Young Women Manual 3*.

Tell them that "evil" spelled backwards is "live." As they "live" the gospel of Jesus Christ, they will gain freedom. Following Jesus Christ leads to liberty, eternal life, and joy.

1. Follow the directions on scripture challenge to learn of those who followed Satan and those who followed Jesus Christ.

2. Observe people or the different countenances on the handout and talk about the peace and joy that radiates from righteous individuals, and the contrast of those who do not make right choices. If time allows, roleplay some of the characters.

COLOR SYMBOL: Color floral symbol on activity and scripture card. File activity in Young Women Valuable Journal behind the value tab.

Choice & Accountability (orange poppy)

PERSONAL PROGRESS* GOALS:
Beehive 1 (Divine Nature 3, Choice & Accountability 4), Beehive 2 (Faith 8), Mia Maid 1 (Choice & Accountability 7, 8, Integrity 4), Mia Maid 2 (Choice & Accountability 5, 8)

THOUGHT TREAT: Memory Mints. Share a bowl of mints with young women and as you enjoy the sweet taste talk about the things we were "mint" to do when we came to earth. Talk about what we "mint" when we said we would follow Jesus and his plan.

MIDWEEK ACTIVITY:
Free Agency Scripture Chase. Have young women organize and compete in a scripture chase, dividing into two teams and racing to find

situations in the scriptures that tell good and bad choices that were made. Tell how this choice affected others. If young women know the stories, ask them to tell them.

❤ Read scriptures to tell a story where someone followed Jesus Christ or chose to follow Satan.

❤ Read how Alma the Younger gave commandments and instruction to his sons Shiblon and Corianton (Alma 38-39).

❤ Talk about the importance of making decisions before the temptations come. This gives us more freedom to choose. We don't have to wait and think about the temptation; we already know what to say and what to do.

❤ (Genesis 37:36; 39) Tell of the example of Joseph in Egypt, who was tempted by his master Potiphar's wife. Tell how Joseph resisted the advances of Potiphar's wife. Talk about Joseph's reaction to her temptation, how he may have decided ahead of time what he would do if he was tempted in this way, because he immediately ran from the situation. If he had hesitated, he may have accepted her request and lost his eternal blessings.

❤ Talk about how we can make those critical choices in our lives.

AGENCY ACTIONS

"For the power is in them, wherein they are agents unto themselves. And inasmuch as men do good they shall in nowise lose their reward."   –D&C 58:28

Out of the scriptures listed below, select two examples who chose to follow Jesus and two examples who chose to follow Satan. Briefly write their story as if you were them.

Mosiah 17:1-4, 18:1-3   Mosiah 11   Alma 53:16-21
Luke 22:47-48   Daniel 6   Genesis 4:1-15
Mosiah 27   1 Nephi 3:28-31   Jacob 7:1-20

Followed Jesus Christ:
Liberty, Eternal Life, Joy

Who: _____
Scripture: _____
_____
_____
_____

Who: _____
Scripture: _____
_____
_____
_____

Followed Satan:
Captivity, Death, Misery

Who: _____
Scripture: _____
_____
_____
_____

Who: _____
Scripture: _____
_____
_____
_____

Lesson #25	**OBEDIENCE:** I Can "Bee" Obedient
	(doorknob hanger with obedience scriptures)

YOU'LL NEED: Copy of doorknob hanger and Thought Treat sign (page 58) on colored cardstock paper for each young woman, pencils, and colored markers.

Review Scripture and teacher summary Handout (page 93) in Young Women Manual 3*.

ACTIVITY: Create a rebus (picture symbol) message "I can be obedient" doorknob hanger to remind young women to be obedient. Remind them of the great blessings that come from obedience.
1. Color and cut out doorknob hanger.
2. Read the scriptures on the doorknob sign, and fill in the blanks to learn about obedience.

PERSONAL PROGRESS* GOALS:
Beehive 1 (Divine Nature 4), Beehive 2 (Divine Nature 3, Choice & Accountability 3, 4, 7), Mia Maid 1 (Choice & Accountability 4)

THOUGHT TREAT: Bee-have Honey Butter Bagels. Mix butter and honey to make a spread for bagels, cutting bagels in half lengthwise.

Buzzzzzz
your way to heaven!

Remind young women that bees are very industrious and they follow Heavenly Father's plan by creating honey. We too can follow his plan for us by obeying his commandments and returning to him. Copy the "Buzz Your Way to Heaven!" sign (page 58) and place it on each half bagel with a toothpick. Poke toothpick through sign or attach toothpick on the back with tape.

MIDWEEK ACTIVITIES:
O"bee"-dient Buzz Session.
1. Have young women bring scriptures and divide

chalkboard into two sides, writing, "Obeyed" on the left and "Disobeyed" on the right.
2. Have young women "buzz" (discuss) people in the scriptures who obeyed (Amulek, Nephi, Naaman, Lehi, Ester, David, Daniel) and people who disobeyed (Lamen and Lemuel, King Noah, and Coriantumer).
3. Write these names on the chalkboard.
4. Discuss the consequences that followed their actions.
5. Talk about people of today who are obedient and who are not (without gossiping or revealing names of friends or family that the others know).
6. Talk about the consequences of their actions.
7. Ask why we risk all that is precious to us and our eternal blessings to be disobedient.

Buzzzzzz
your way to heaven!

OBEDIENCE

Search the scriptures to learn about OBEDIENCE:

Jeremiah 7:23-24
"_ _ _ _ _ _ ye in all the ways that I have commanded."

D&C 130:18-21
"[Any] blessing from God ... is by obedience to that _ _ _ _."

D&C 59:23
"Who doeth ... righteousness shall receive his _ _ _ _ _ _ _ _ _, even _ _ _ _ _ _ _ _ in this world, and eternal life in the world to come."

D&C 82:8-10
"I, the Lord, am _ _ _ _ _ _ _ _ when ye do what I say."

John 14:15, 21
"If ye _ _ _ _ _ _ me, _ _ _ _ _ _ my commandments."

1 Corinthians 2:9
"God hath prepared [great things] for them that _ _ _ _ _ _ him."

| **Lesson #26** | **REPENTANCE: I Will Change My Thoughts and Behavior**
(D&C 18:13 tent card challenge) |

YOU'LL NEED: Copy of tent card challenge (page 60) on colored cardstock paper for each young woman, pencils, and markers.

ACTIVITY:
Help young women memorize D&C 18:13 and talk about the joy that comes to the soul when one repents.

> *Review Preparation #2 (page 94) and Lesson Application (page 96) in Young Women Manual 3*.*

1. Color, cut out, and fold tent card to stand up.
2. Write things you want to change in your thoughts and actions on tent card.
3. Talk of great men and women who repented and found joy, like Alma the Younger (Mosiah 27). Alma the Younger and his friends, the sons of Mosiah, were promised eternal life (Mosiah 28:1-9).
4. Talk about the repentance process we must go through, as Alma the Younger did (Alma 36:16-21).
5. Talk about people in our personal lives who made spiritual changes.

COLOR SYMBOL: Color floral symbol on activity and scripture card. File activity in Young Women Value-able Journal behind the value tab.

> *Choice & Accountability (orange poppy)*

PERSONAL PROGRESS* GOALS:
Beehive 1 (Integrity 1),
Beehive 2 (Integrity 3),
Mia Maid 1 (Integrity 1),
Mia Maid 2 (Choice & Accountability 7)

THOUGHT TREAT: Repentance Fruit Roll-ups. Give each young woman a piece of fruit leather rolled up with a string attached, or inside a package. Tell them that before they "roll" into bed at night, think of things they may have done during the day that they need to repent of, and ask Heavenly Father for forgiveness. Then before they "roll" out of bed in the morning, pray that they can keep the commandments.

MIDWEEK ACTIVITIES:
1. **Mighty Change of Heart.** Tell young women: "You can never really change until you change your heart! A changed heart is a repentant heart." Talk about the mighty change of heart in the Book of Mormon. Have a special skit dramatizing a story in the Book of Mormon, e.g., Alma the Younger. Serve heart-shaped cupcakes or heart-shaped pancakes with strawberry syrup, strawberries and whipped cream. Make notes on hearts and then stick them on dozens of cars in the church parking Sunday or on the mailbox of a special friend.
2. Inner and Outer Beauty Personality Plus Workshop. Focus on the positive, asking young women and young women leaders to bring ideas to share that will help us look on the bright side.

Ideas
Practice smiling three times a day, greet the day with a song, look for reasons to be happy, read the scriptures daily, pray for guidance in your decisions, repent of wrongdoings, and resolve to change. Begin by changing your thoughts.

How to Change Your Thoughts
It just takes 15 seconds to change your negative impression into a positive thought. Take the first five seconds to decide that you do not want that negative thought to enter your mind. Then take the next five seconds to think of a positive thought. Take the last five seconds to repeat that positive thought in your mind.

Things I will change in my
Thoughts and actions:

Actions

Thoughts

And how great
is his JOY in
the soul that
repenteth!

D&C
18:13

Lesson #27*　　　**FORGIVENESS: I Will Forgive Myself and Others**
(mirror message poster)

YOU'LL NEED: Copy of Forgive Yourself poster (page 62) for each young woman on colored cardstock paper, scissors, and colored markers.

Review Scripture discussion D&C 88:33 (page 99) in Young Women Manual 3*.

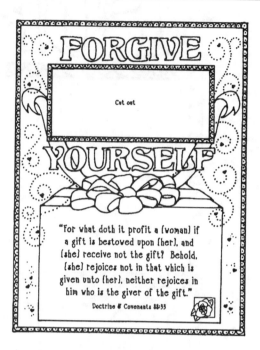

ACTIVITY: Tell young women self-love is a gift you can give yourself through the repentance and forgiving process. Read Alma the Younger's story of repentance and forgiveness (Alma 36:16-21).

1. Color the Forgive Yourself poster.
2. Cut out the box where indicated.
3. Read the D&C 88:33 scripture on the poster.
4. Hold the poster up to your face as you look into a mirror. While peering through the poster, tell yourself that you forgive yourself for the wrong choices you have made.
5. Tell yourself how you will change.
6. Tell young women to imagine this box as a television set within our mind. When we put a scene or experience in our mind and run it over and over again, we are not letting the sin go. After we repent of a sin, we should never have re-runs!

COLOR SYMBOL: Color floral symbol on activity and scripture card. File activity in Young Women Value-able Journal behind the value tab.

Individual Worth (red rose)

PERSONAL PROGRESS* GOALS:
Beehive 2 (Individual Worth 3, 4, 8),
Mia Maid 1 (Choice & Accountability 6)

THOUGHT TREAT: Tear Drop Candy Kisses. Give each young woman several candy kisses. Tell them that these teardrop-shaped candies remind us of the tears Jesus shed when he suffered for our sins. They remind us of the tears our parents shed when we turn away from the teachings of Jesus. They remind us of the

tears we shed as we repent of our sins. Conclude with, " Now think of them as candy kisses. Let's forgive ourselves and give ourselves a kiss as we change and forsake our sins."

MIDWEEK ACTIVITY:
Letting Go!
1. Write on a piece of paper something you did that was wrong or unkind, etc. Do not include your name.
2. Fold the paper and place it on a helium balloon or around a stick or in a pinecone.
3. Then have a ceremony and talk about forgiveness and the healing power it has. Have an older girl (Laurel) give a talk about "Letting go of negative and unkind actions."
4. Have a silent prayer where girls can ask for forgiveness if they haven't already, and ask Heavenly Father to help you release these feelings.
5. Then let go of the balloons all at once, or go to a river and watch the sticks float away, or stand around a campfire and throw in your pine cones.
6. Resolve to never do that again. Take a deep breath and forgive and let it go!

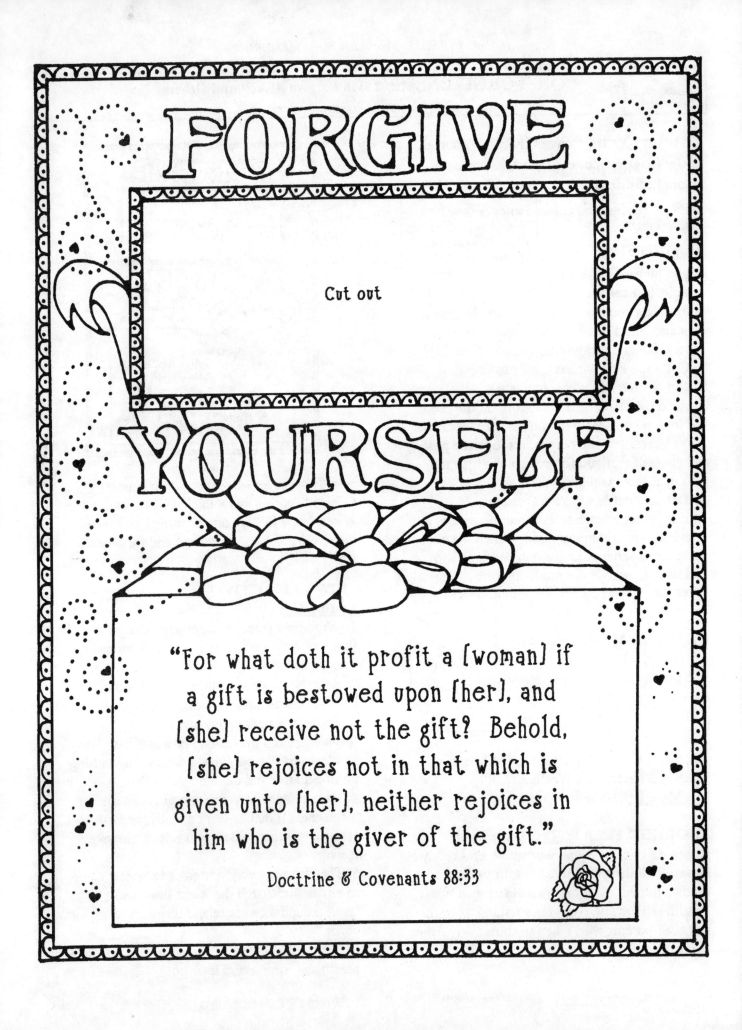

FORGIVE

Cut out

YOURSELF

"For what doth it profit a [woman] if a gift is bestowed upon [her], and [she] receive not the gift? Behold, [she] rejoices not in that which is given unto [her], neither rejoices in him who is the giver of the gift."

Doctrine & Covenants 88:33

Lesson #28	**CONSECRATION & SACRIFICE:** I Will Sacrifice My Time,
	Talents, and Means to Build Up the Kingdom of God
	(Mosiah 2:34 sacrifice tent card)

YOU'LL NEED: Copy of tent card (page 64) on colored cardstock paper for each young woman, pencils, and colored markers.

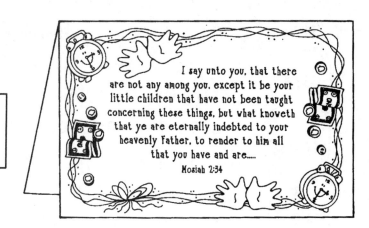

I say unto you, that there are not any among you, except it be your little children that have not been taught concerning these things, but what knoweth that ye are eternally indebted to your heavenly Father, to render to him all that you have and are.....
Mosiah 2:34

ACTIVITY:

Review Preparation #1 (page 100) and Conclusion Teacher presentation (page 103) in Young Women Manual 3*.

To remind young women of King Benjamin's address to the Nephites on the law of sacrifice and consecration, create this bite-size memorize and tent card.

1. Color and memorize scripture tent card.

2. Write three ways you can build up the kingdom of God by giving of your TIME, your TALENTS, and your MEANS. EXAMPLES: TIME: Tending children while parents attend the temple or elders quorum party. Help Primary leaders with handouts and visuals to use during Primary sharing time. Create toys for Primary nursery. Read and present special activities to the Primary nursery. TALENTS: Bake bread for a neighbor, clean an elderly person's home, help them organize, offer friendship. MEANS: Use your babysitting money to buy flowers for the elderly. Pay your tithing. Add extra money to the mission fund or fast offerings.

COLOR SYMBOL: Color floral symbol on activity and scripture card. File activity in Young Women Value-able Journal behind the value tab.

Good Works (yellow sunflower)

PERSONAL PROGRESS* GOALS:
Beehive 1 (Divine Nature 2, Individual Worth 4, Knowledge 1, 5, Choice & Accountability 3, Good Works 2, 3), Beehive 2 (Individual Worth 6, Good Works 5, 6), Mia Maid 1 (Knowledge 3), Laurel 1 & 2 Project #3 (page 79)

THOUGHT TREAT: <u>Cookies for a Neighbor</u>.
1. Make and share a batch of cookies for young women to sample.
2. Ask young women to make and deliver a batch of cookies for a neighbor who is a nonmember or someone in need of fellowship.
3. Tell them that this is one way they can build up the kingdom of God by sharing their TIME, TALENTS, and MEANS.

MIDWEEK ACTIVITIES:
<u>Count Your Blessings Service Fun.</u>
Tell young women, when you serve someone less fortunate than you, you not only feel good about serving, but you count your blessings! Suggest and do one or more of the following:
♥ clean up after a ward dinner
♥ read to or teach children skills
♥ have an elf night, leaving notes, packages, or treats anonymously
♥ visit the elderly often to cheer and offer assistance
♥ visit a nursing home on holidays, bearing cards and gifts
♥ read to the elderly and share your favorite classical music
♥ help the handicapped.

I say unto you, that there
are not any among you, except it be your
little children that have not been taught
concerning these things, but what knoweth
that ye are eternally indebted to your
heavenly father, to render to him all
that you have and are......

Mosiah 2:34

How I can build up the kingdom of God
by giving of my:

Time:_____

Talents:_____

Means:_____

Lesson #29   **CHANGE OF HEART:** I Will Be Faithful in Keeping the Commandments

(My Change of Heart mobile)

YOU'LL NEED: Copy of the My Change of Heart mobile (pages 66-67) on colored cardstock paper for each young woman, pencils, string, and colored markers. **OPTION:** Copy mobile pattern on two different colors of cardstock paper so when mobile turns, one side will be a different color from the other side.

ACTIVITY: Create a two-sided mobile to show young women the four steps King Benjamin's people

Review the Review steps #1-4 (page 105) in Young Women Manual 3*.

went through to have a change of heart (Mosiah 5:2, 5). "My Change of Heart Steps:

Step #1: I will learn about Christ and his commandments.

Step #2: I will have faith in Christ and believe in his Atonement.

Step #3: I will ask for forgiveness, and be forgiven through the Lord's mercy.

Step #4: I will make a covenant to keep the commandments, and do good all my days."

TO CREATE MOBILE: (1) Copy mobile on two different colors (see above option). (2) Color and cut out hearts. (3) Lay My Change of Heart Steps #1-2 pieces ½-inch apart face down. (4) Place a 2-inch piece of string down the center, taping the string to the #1-2 pieces on the blank side. (5) Lay and glue steps #3-4 and Mosiah 5:2, 5 pieces face up over the matching steps #1-2 pieces. Make sure the long piece of the string is at the top to hang mobile. Mobile pieces can turn with string, giving a different message that could match the one on the other side if turned around. NOTE: If you create this mobile in different colors, it will be easier to see the right message as mobile turns.

PERSONAL PROGRESS* GOALS:
Beehive 1 (Faith 4), Beehive 2 (Faith 1), Mia Maid 1 (Divine Nature 7)

THOUGHT TREAT: Change of Heart Cupcakes. Top frosted cupcakes with four pieces of candy, and as you eat, review the four steps to have a change of heart (shown above).

MIDWEEK ACTIVITIES:
1. Tug at the Heart Strings. Have an evening of poetry reading at someone's house and feel those heart strings tug. Use soft lights and music to set a relaxed mood. Also read selected scriptures that show heart-felt emotion. Encourage young women to really think about this and come prepared with their favorite poetry, hymns, or scriptures to read.

2. Change of Heart Role Play. Have young women team up and visit the ward library to find an article that expresses a change of heart. Have them rehearse and then act out the story in a 5-minute play for the other young women. Act while one person reads parts of the story.

My Change of ♥ Steps

1. I will learn about Christ

and learn of his commandments.

2. I will have faith in Christ

and believe in his Atonement.

My Change of ♥ Steps

3. I will ask for forgiveness

and be forgiven through
the Lord's mercy.

4. I will make a covenant to
keep the commandments,

and do good all
my days.

Lesson #30	**SCRIPTURE STUDY:** I Love to Read the Scriptures
	(scripture challenge bookmark with testimony journal)

YOU'LL NEED: Copy of a bookmark (page 69) on colored cardstock paper for each young woman, scissors, glue, and colored markers.

ACTIVITY:

> *Review Lesson Application (page 110) in Young Women Manual 3*.*

Remind young women to read the scriptures daily.

1. <u>Create a Bookmark</u>. Color and cut out bookmark, fold, and glue back-to-back.

2. <u>Motivate Scripture Reading</u>. For next week, challenge young women to read the scripture assigned on the bookmark each day. After they read the scripture, draw a heart ♥ in box. In the space below, write key words from the scripture to motivate you to read the scriptures.

3. <u>Challenge Personal Study</u>. Challenge young women to start or continue a personal scripture study program, and pray for the Spirit of the Holy Ghost to guide them as they read.

4. <u>Encourage Testimony</u>. Ask them to write their testimony on side two of the bookmark.

5. <u>Laminate Bookmark</u>. When steps #1-4 are completed, laminate bookmark to place in their scriptures.

COLOR SYMBOL: Color floral symbol on activity and scripture card. File activity in Young Women Value-able Journal behind the value tab.

Knowledge (green ivy)

PERSONAL PROGRESS* GOALS:
<u>Beehive 1</u> (Knowledge 6, 7), <u>Beehive 2</u> (Knowledge 2), <u>Mia Maid 2</u> (Good Works 4), <u>Laurel 1 & 2</u> Project #6 (page 79)

THOUGHT TREAT: <u>String Licorice</u>. To match with Activity #2 (right), tie different colors of licorice strings together. Tell young women that the scriptures are full of a string of stories that all tie into the gospel of Jesus Christ.

MIDWEEK ACTIVITIES:

1. String of Scripture Stories. With two different colored packages of yarn, cut yarn into different size lengths and tie together, e.g., tie white yarn to pink yarn. Wind yarn into a ball. Ask young women to pass the ball around, with the person before them unwinding the string slowly (an inch per five seconds), while the person in front starts a scripture story. When the person gets to the next knot, the yarn is passed on and the next young woman who continues the story, or starts a new story.

2. Scripture Bowl. Have a bowl filled with scriptures and scripture questions. Young women can divide into teams and race to find the answer, taking turns drawing the question. The first team to find and read the answer wins! Examples: Who was King Benjamin's father? How do I know if the Book of Mormon is true? (see Moroni 10:4-5). FUN OPTION: Have dads or bishopric team up with or compete with young women to find the answers.

OPTION: Young women can come with 10 of their favorite scriptures to share in the scripture chase.

PATTERN: SCRIPTURE STUDY (bookmark/journal)

I love to read the Scriptures!

Sun
☐ 2 Nephi 4:15

Mon
☐ Matt. 22:29

Tues
☐ 2 Tim. 3:15

Wed
☐ John 5:39

Thur
☐ Jacob 7:19

Fri
☐ Luke 24:32

Sat
☐ D&C 26:1

After reading the scripture for the day, draw a ♡ in the box.

This week I will start or continue my Personal Scripture Study Program.

My testimony: _____

_____

_____

_____

_____

_____

_____

_____

_____

_____

_____

_____

_____

| Lesson #31 | **SERVICE IN THE CHURCH:** I Will Serve the Lord |
| | *(L.D.S. PRESS interview tools)* |

YOU'LL NEED: Copy of interview journal, appreciation card, and L.D.S. PRESS tag on colored cardstock paper (pages 71-72) for each young woman, pencils, and colored markers.

ACTIVITY:

> Review Lesson Application #3 (page 114) in Young Women Manual 3*.

To help young women gain a clearer understanding and appreciation of those who serve the Lord. Get ready for a midweek activity to interview someone who has served in the Church (for example: presidents, counselors, teachers, nursery leader, ward librarian, bishop, deacon, teacher, music, and priest leaders).

1. Use the Service Interview Journal to take notes during the interview.
2. Go in groups of two or more and call ahead for the interview.
3. Carry a fake microphone, wear a hat with L.D.S. PRESS on top, or wear as a name tag.
4. On Sunday, make a list of interview questions: What is your calling in the church? How long have you served in this calling? What do you do in this calling? How do you feel about this calling? Share your experiences and feelings."
4. You could call yourself the _____ Ward Newsies. Possibly some of the interviews could be placed in the ward newsletter, after receiving permission from the bishop and each person interviewed.
5. Talk about the interviews, sharing information.
6. Ask young women to send a Note of Appreciation to the person interviewed, expressing their thanks for the interview and for serving in their church calling.

COLOR SYMBOL: Color floral symbol on activity and scripture card. File activity in Young Women Value-able Journal behind the value tab.

Good Works (yellow sunflower)

Service Interview Journal

Person who has served: _____
Position: _____
What do you enjoy about your calling? _____

What is difficult about your calling? _____

What knowledge would you pass on to others? _____

How did it increase your testimony? _____

PERSONAL PROGRESS* GOALS:
Beehive 1 (Individual Worth 2, Knowledge 8, Good Works 1, 7, Integrity 6), Mia Maid 1 (Knowledge 4, Good Works 2, 7, 8), Mia Maid 2 (Faith 1, Good Works 3, 5-8)

THOUGHT TREAT: Called to Serve Soda. Make a 3" round smile face sign with the words CALLED TO SERVE: I Will Serve the Lord" written in the border. Punch two holes at the top and bottom and attach this sign to a straw. Place the straw in a can of soda pop for each young woman. Tell them that service brings a smile. When we are called to serve, if we serve the best we can with a smile, we will grow in spirit, just as this soda pop rises to the top when we shake the can or sip the soda with a straw.

MIDWEEK ACTIVITIES
1. **Service Interview.** See Activity (left) #1-5.
2. **Bishop Talk.** Ask the bishop to tell about his calling as a bishop, how his counselors help him, and how he calls members of the ward to serve in Church callings.

*Young Women Manual 3 and Personal Progress books are published by The Church of Jesus Christ of Latter-day Saints, Salt Lake City, Utah.

Service Interview Journal

Person who has served: _____
Position: _____
What do you enjoy about your calling? _____
_____
_____

What is difficult about your calling? _____
_____
_____

What knowledge would you pass on to others? _____
_____
_____
_____

How did it increase your testimony? _____
_____
_____
_____

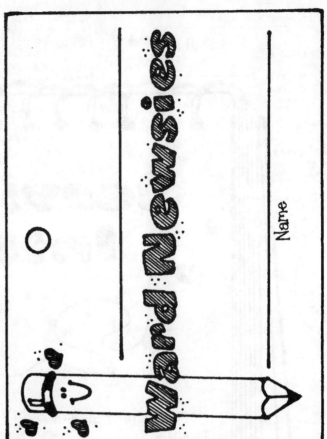

Happy Memories

Name _____

Just a
little
note of
THANKS

Lesson #32   **SERVICE IN THE COMMUNITY:** I Will Take the Time to Serve
(Community Service Project Planner)

YOU'LL NEED: Copy of the Community Service Project Planner form (page 74) for each young woman, pencils, and colored markers.

ACTIVITY:

> *Review Map Activity and Lesson Application #1 (page 117) in Young Women Manual 3*.*

1. Encourage young women to take the time to serve others in their community.
2. As a group or as two individuals, decide on a community service project. Ask young women to use this Project Planner form to plan what they will do.
3. First check the type of service they will perform in one of the four boxes.
4. Write the name of the service project, the schedule, and whom they served with.
5. Perform the service and write about your experience in the journal space provided.

COLOR SYMBOL: Color floral symbol on activity and scripture card. File activity in Young Women Valueable Journal behind the value tab.

> *Good Works (yellow sunflower)*

PERSONAL PROGRESS* GOALS:
Beehive 1 (Knowledge 3, Good Works 8, 9), Beehive 2 (Knowledge 3, 4, Good Works 2, 3), Mia Maid 1 (Knowledge 5, Good Works 3, 4, 5), Mia Maid 2 (Knowledge 8, Good Works 1, 2, Integrity 7), Laurel 1 & 2 Projects #4, 10, and 11-17 (page 79)

THOUGHT TREAT: String Licorice Game. Purchase two packages of string licorice (for 10 young women) and play this fun game to brainstorm community service ideas. See #6 shown right.

Go the Extra Mile String Licorice Game.
TO CREATE GAME: Type up a list of service ideas gathered by young women or found in your local library or community service column in the local newspaper. Cut ideas into individual idea wordstrips. On 15 separate slips of paper, write numbers 1, 2, 3, 4, or 5. Fold all idea and number wordstrips in one container.

TO PLAY GAME:

1. Divide young women into two teams. Have teams take turns drawing a wordstrip from the pile of combined service ideas and numbers 1-5.
2. If they draw a service idea, tell others how they might perform this community service. They can then collect one string of licorice.
3. If they draw a number, e.g. "5," they name five service projects needed in a community, and collect five strings of licorice for their team.
4. The team with the most strings of licorice win.
5. OPTION: Tie the licorice strings together and at the end; instead of counting the number of strings, stretch it across the room to see who has the longest string. Say, "We will go the extra mile to serve in our community."
6. Ask young women to stretch the piece of licorice and think about stretching their talents as they serve.

MIDWEEK ACTIVITY: Service Project Brainstorm: Have young women think up service ideas and vote on those you can do together (see Personal Progress above).

Young Women Manual 3 and Personal Progress books are published by The Church of Jesus Christ of Latter-day Saints, Salt Lake City, Utah.

Community Service
PROJECT PLANNER

Project I chose:_____
_____

Type of Service:_____
_____

Contact Person:_____ Phone:_____
Date of Project:_____ Time:_____
Location:_____
Who will be involved:_____
_____
_____
_____

Supplies Needed:_____
_____

Notes:_____
_____

Journal of My Experience:

_____
_____
_____
_____
_____
_____
_____

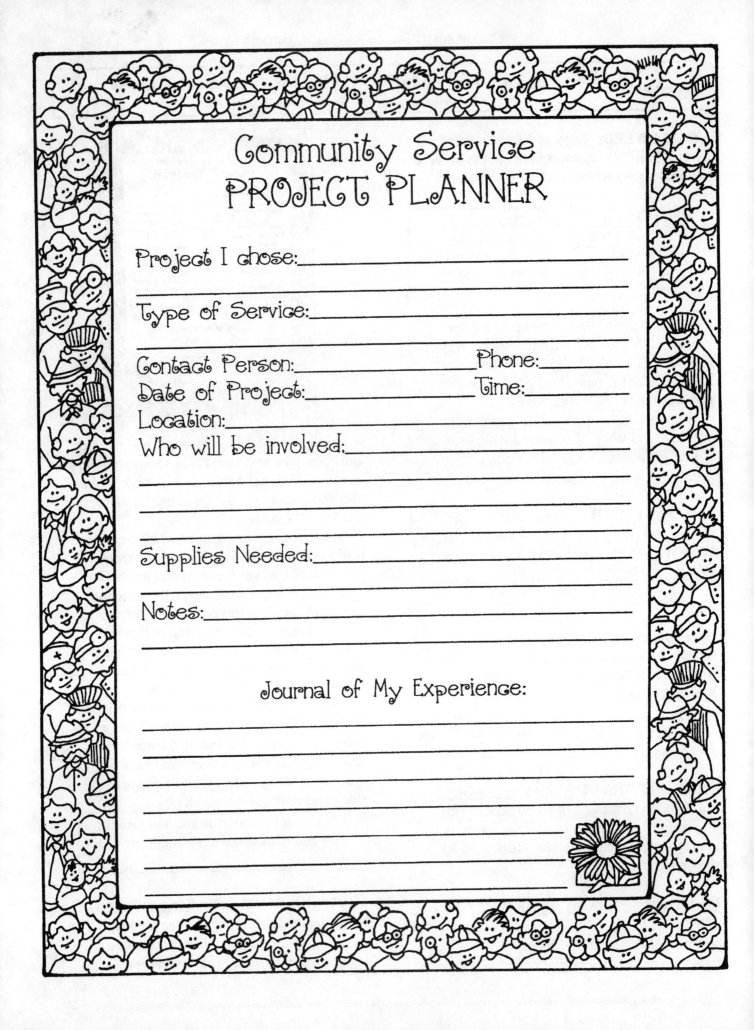

Lesson #33 **FRIENDSHIP:** Each Person Is Divine and Eternal
(Friend-ship Anchors in an eternal lifeboat)

YOU'LL NEED: Copy of eternal lifeboat, Friend-"ship" Anchor wordstrips (pages 76-77) for each young woman, scissors, glue, pencils, and markers.

ACTIVITY: Talk about friendship being an anchor, something that holds our boat steady in times of trouble. Help young women learn ways to be an anchor or offer friendship and love to someone who needs support (especially if there is a less-active member in the class or an investigator). Challenge young women to take these Friend-"ship" Anchor wordstrips to serve as reminders.

> *Review Preparation #3 (page 120) and Lesson Applications #1 and #2 (page 121) in Young Women Manual 3*.*

1. Color and cut out boat and Friend-"ship" Anchors.
2. Fold and glue boat on the rounded edge 1/4", leaving room for a pocket.
3. Insert wordstrips inside boat.
4. In class ask young women to take turns pulling out a wordstrip (from one boat), and read the challenge. Tell why it is important, or share a personal experience.
5. Read the following scriptures on friendship: 1 Samuel 16:7, Matthew 25:40, Romans 12:10, and Doctrine and Covenants 18:10.
6. Encourage young women to do this activity with their family.

COLOR SYMBOL: Color floral symbol on activity and scripture card. File activity in Young Women Value-able Journal behind the value tab.

> *Good Works (yellow sunflower)*

PERSONAL PROGRESS* GOALS:
Beehive 1 (Divine Nature 1),
Beehive 2 (Divine Nature 8, Good Works 7, Integrity 7),
Mia Maid 1 (Individual Worth 4, 9, Integrity 6)

Ahoy young women mates! Here are some friendship anchors to keep your friend-ship sailing, for ... nd-ships are never ending.

THE FRIEND-SHIP
If you were in the same boat needing an eternal friend, what would you need on your journey, and on whom would you depend?

THOUGHT TREAT: FRIEND-"SHIP" Banana Boats. Share with young woman a banana boat treat they can create themselves. Cut a banana in half lengthwise. Dig out the center with a spoon and add chocolate chips, caramel, fudge, and miniature marshmallows. Top with two maraschino cherries to represent friends. Enjoy the treat as you talk about keeping their friends' eternal boat afloat (by being a good influence).

MIDWEEK ACTIVITIES:
1. Put Yourself in Her Shoes. Have each young woman choose another young woman in the ward or at school, then talk to her and find out all about her. She can also talk to her mom or sister and find out her likes, dislikes, fears, and talents. Then when you meet, have young women tell the class about themselves as if they were the other girl, e.g., "I hate spiders. I have the coolest brother. My sister died at age three," etc. Then talk about how you can be better friends when you understand and feel empathy.
2. Pal Pet Peeves. Brainstorm your likes and dislikes concerning friendships. Ideas will help young women in developing future friendships.

THE FRIEND-SHIP

If you were in the same boat
needing an eternal friend,
what would you need on your journey,
and on whom would you depend?

Ahoy young women mates!
Here are some friend-ship anchors
to keep your friend-ship sailing
for true friend-ships are never ending.

FRIEND-"SHIP" ANCHORS: Say hello and smile each time you see me.

FRIEND-"SHIP" ANCHORS: Go the extra mile to find answers to my questions.

FRIEND-"SHIP" ANCHORS: Show interest. Ask me what I like to do.

FRIEND-"SHIP" ANCHORS: Encourage me to seek friends with good values.

FRIEND-"SHIP" ANCHORS: Compliment me if I look nice or do something you like.

FRIEND-"SHIP" ANCHORS: Invite me to work on Personal Progress goals with you.

FRIEND-"SHIP" ANCHORS: Call me; don't wait for me to call you.

FRIEND-"SHIP" ANCHORS: Invite me to church meetings and Young Women activities.

FRIEND-"SHIP" ANCHORS: Be positive. Act as if I like you, even though I don't show you that I like you.

FRIEND-"SHIP" ANCHORS: Read the scriptures and *Era* with me.

FRIEND-"SHIP" ANCHORS: Be yourself around me.

FRIEND-"SHIP" ANCHORS: Introduce me to your value-able friends.

FRIEND-"SHIP" ANCHORS: Get to know my parents. Talk to them.

FRIEND-"SHIP" ANCHORS: Have a surprise party for me when it's my birthday.

FRIEND-"SHIP" ANCHORS: Send me a card or note anytime.

FRIEND-"SHIP" ANCHORS: Invite me to do things with your family.

FRIEND-"SHIP" ANCHORS: Make time for me by inviting me to whatever you are doing.

FRIEND-"SHIP" ANCHORS: Give me pointers in dress and grooming, tactfully.

FRIEND-"SHIP" ANCHORS: Chat about what is important to you.

FRIEND-"SHIP" ANCHORS: Answer my questions about the gospel.

FRIEND-"SHIP" ANCHORS: Listen to what is important to me.

FRIEND-"SHIP" ANCHORS: Write encouraging notes to motivate me to make right choices.

Lesson #34

HONESTY: I Will Avoid Dishonesty and Its Consequences
(Are You Miss Honest or Dishonest Consequences Journal)

YOU'LL NEED: Copy of journal (page 78) for each young woman, pencils, and markers.

ACTIVITY: Help decide if they are "Miss Honest or Dishonest" with this Consequences Journal. With this journal young women can think about the consequences of honest and dishonest choices. Consider how this action will affect your life by writing in detail the consequences for each decision. Example: The consequence for stealing is that people won't trust you.

> *Review Quotation (page 123), and Dishonesty Has Many Negative Consequences (page 123-124) in Young Women Manual 3*.*

COLOR SYMBOL: Color floral symbol on activity and scripture card. File activity in Young Women Value-able Journal behind the value tab.

Integrity (purple pansy)

Are you **Miss Honest** or **Dishonest?** Consequences Journal

Action	Consequence
Dressing Modestly:	
Gossiping:	
Coveting:	
Speaking the Truth:	
Borrowing Things:	
Stealing:	
Making a Promise:	
Paying a Full Tithing:	

PERSONAL PROGRESS* GOALS:
Beehive 1 (Integrity 6), Beehive 2 (Integrity 1), Mia Maid 1 (Integrity 2, 5)

THOUGHT TREAT: Consequence Cookies.
1. Frost two cookies for each young woman, one with a smile and the other with a frown.
2. As you eat, talk about the actions that might bring happiness to you and our Heavenly Father, making him smile.
3. Talk about the actions that would bring a frown or unhappiness.
4. You could make two different batches of cookies, adding salt instead of sugar to the frown cookies, and the right ingredients to the smile cookies.
5. When young women eat the frown cookie, remind them of the bitter taste of dishonesty and the sweet taste of honesty.
6. When they eat the smile cookie, talk about the peaceful feelings and blessings that come from making honest choices.

MIDWEEK ACTIVITIES:

1. Covenants and Promises.

☺ Quote Joshua 24:15 "Choose you this day whom ye will serve, but as for me and my house, we will serve the Lord."

☺ Talk about the Young Women motto: "Stand for Truth and Righteousness."

☺ Talk about the "Times," "Things," and "Places" where we make covenants and promises. "Times" of Our Lives: Youth, missions, college, marriage, motherhood. "Things" in Our Lives: Callings, jobs, careers, responsibilities. "Places" in Our Lives: Movie theater, school, mall, dates, vacations, store, library, recreational sites.

2. Situation Preview. Look ahead at situations that may happen in our lives and what we will do to make honest decisions. Project what the consequences might be with both an honest and dishonest decision. Make decisions now to say "no," keeping in mind the straight and narrow path that leads back to our Heavenly Father.

Are you

Miss Honest
or
Dishonest?
Consequences Journal

Action	Consequence
Dressing Modestly:	
Gossiping:	
Coveting:	
Speaking the Truth:	
Borrowing Things:	
Stealing:	
Making a Promise:	
Paying a Full Tithing:	

DATING DECISIONS: My Dating Decisions Affect My Eternal Life

Lesson #35

*(*My BIG Dating Decisions poster*)*

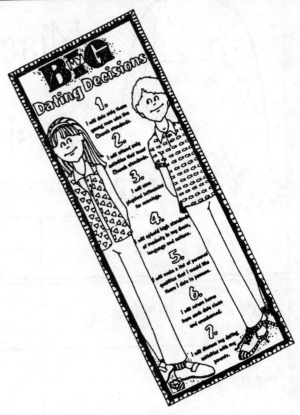

YOU'LL NEED: Copy of poster (pages 81-82) for each young woman, pencils, and markers.

ACTIVITY: Young women use this BIG Dating Decisions poster to serve as reminders as they make their big dating decisions. Remind young women that each dating decision can impact her eternal life in the celestial kingdom with Heavenly Father and Jesus. To make poster, glue parts A and B together and color. Encourage young women to post this in their room.

> *Review Chalkboard discussion (page 128) in Young Women Manual 3*.*

COLOR SYMBOL: Color floral symbol on activity and scripture card. File activity in Young Women Value-able Journal behind the value tab.

Choice & Accountability (orange poppy)

PERSONAL PROGRESS* GOALS:
Mia Maid 2 (Choice & Accountability 1, 2)

THOUGHT TREAT: Eternal Lifesavers. Share with each young woman seven Lifesavers candies (hard or gummy type candies) and say, "The seven BIG decisions you make here this day, shown on this poster, will affect your marriage eternally. Look at the ring shape of this candy and think of the wedding ring that you will wear someday. The decisions you make now and each day will affect the quality of life you will have in the eternities." After reading the poster together, read Jacob 6:11, and 2 Nephi 2:27-29 and 10:23 to motivate these eternal life decisions.

MIDWEEK ACTIVITIES:
1. Date for Mr. Right. Talk to young women about dating each young man as if their dates would someday be on video for their future mates to see. Tell them to date with the real purpose in mind (eternal marriage), to date as

though their future posterity (children) were watching.
2. List Pitfalls to Avoid: Single dates, being alone with the opposite sex, dating nonmembers, dating someone who is into drinking, etc. Observe how their date treats his mother (a reflection on how he will someday treat his wife), observe how he feels about the Church, a mission, etc. Have young women ask themselves, is he polite and considerate, what does he like to do with his time, etc.
3. Sneak Preview. Ahead of time (a week earlier) have the young men write down anonymously their ideal girl (what they like and don't like in a date or future mate).
4. Videos and Recordings on Dating and future choices are available at the Church Distribution Center and LDS bookstores. Have a check-out system where each young woman can review these privately during the week if time does not allow you to show them all.
5. Review LDS Books on Dating.

*Young Women Manual 3 and Personal Progress books are published by The Church of Jesus Christ of Latter-day Saints, Salt Lake City, Utah.

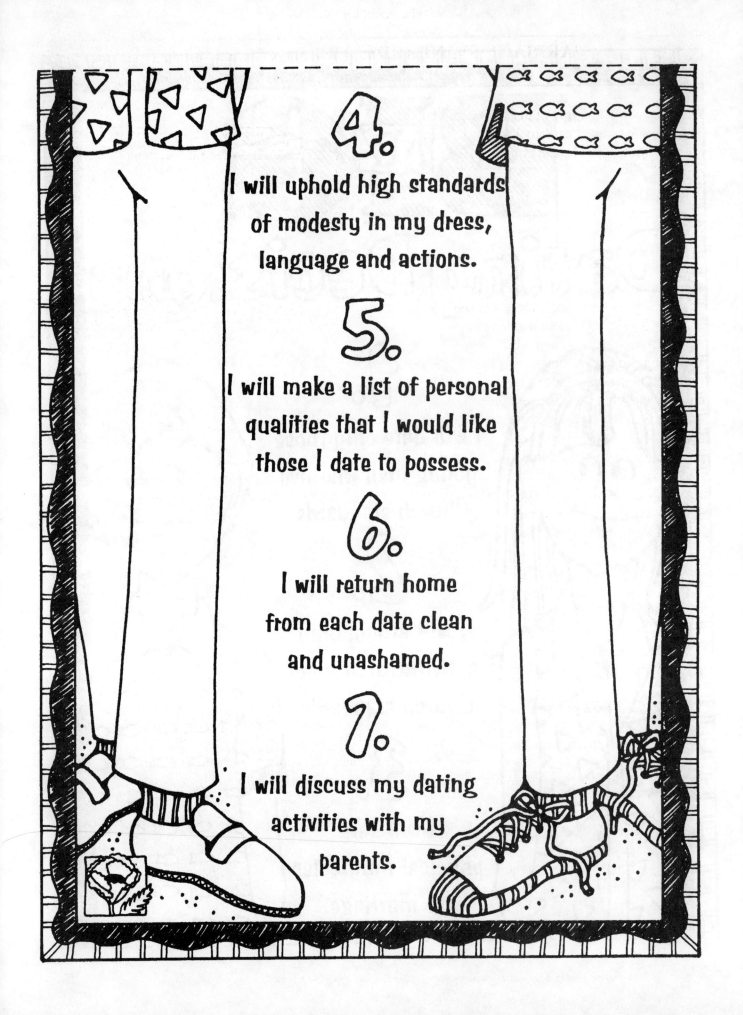

4.

I will uphold high standards of modesty in my dress, language and actions.

5.

I will make a list of personal qualities that I would like those I date to possess.

6.

I will return home from each date clean and unashamed.

7.

I will discuss my dating activities with my parents.

MARRIAGE STANDARDS: I Will Make Eternal Marriage Decisions

Lesson #36

(Positive Traits to Attract a Positive Mate! decision tent card)

YOU'LL NEED: Copy of decision tent card (page 84) on colored cardstock paper for each young woman, pencils, and colored markers.

ACTIVITY:
Color, cut out, and fold tent card.

Review Preparation #3 (page 129), and Activity (pages 130 and 131) in Young Women Manual 3*.

Step #1: Looking on one side of the tent card, help young women memorize the "Marriage is perhaps the most vital of all decisions" quote from Spencer W. Kimball, and talk about making that important decision now and when the opportunity to marry comes.

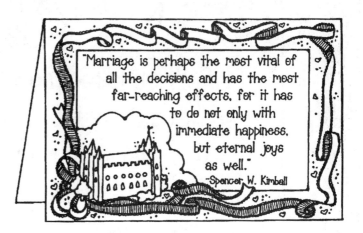

Step #2: On the other side of the tent card, have young women list the positive traits they would like in their future marriage partner. Then also list what they want to be. This list could be the same qualities they would like to develop. Remind young women that if they want to date and marry a person with the qualities they desire, they too must acquire these qualities. This way they will attract that type of individual to them.

COLOR-CODE JOURNAL:
Color floral symbol on activity and scripture card. File activity in Young Women Value Journal behind the value tab.

Individual Worth (red rose)

PERSONAL PROGRESS* GOALS:
Beehive 1 (Divine Nature 5),
Beehive 2 (Individual Worth 1)

THOUGHT TREAT: Sweet Dates. Give each young woman two dates (pieces of dried fruit) or trail mix or cookies with dates in them. Ask them as they eat this sweet fruit to think of the rich experiences they can have during their dating years if they remember the standards they have set for themselves and for those they date.

MIDWEEK ACTIVITIES:
1. Panel Discussion on Dating: Ask several individuals from another ward (who have been recommended by their bishop) to answer questions on dating and gospel standards. Many of the questions can be taken from Lesson #35 (page 128—#1-7 guidelines). Ask young men and women from your ward to write down their dating questions ahead of time.

2. "My Man" Wish List. Have young women brainstorm about what kind of man they would like to marry. Make this a long list. Then check all the ones that really matter the most, crossing out or erasing the not-so-necessary qualifications. Last, ask the girls if they think they themselves possess these traits. Then explain that we can't expect something of someone if we are not willing to be that too.

3. Look Ahead Decisions. Talk about dating decisions and how to say "yes" and "no." Saying "yes" is easy if you like someone, but saying "no" can be a challenge, especially if we have promised to live the Church standards and keep our lives morally clean. Talk about situations that may come up and how to handle each. You are using your head if you look "ahead."

"Marriage is perhaps the most vital of all the decisions and has the most far-reaching effects, for it has to do not only with immediate happiness, but eternal joys as well."

-Spencer W. Kimball

POSITIVE TRAITS to ATTRACT A POSITIVE MATE!

I want him to be:

♥ _____
♥ _____
♥ _____
♥ _____
♥ _____
♥ _____

I want to be:

♥ _____
♥ _____
♥ _____
♥ _____
♥ _____
♥ _____

Lesson #37	STANDARDS: I Can Cope with World Philosophies as I Live Gospel Standards *(Gospel Standard Word Find)*

YOU'LL NEED: Copy of Gospel Standards Word Find (page 86) on colored cardstock paper for each young woman, pencils, and colored markers.

ACTIVITY: Read John 14:27 *"My peace I give unto you: not as the world giveth."* Explain that Jesus sent us the Holy Ghost, the Comforter, to speak to our hearts and minds as we live the gospel standards. This is a peace that we need in this troubled world. Help young women review their gospel standards—how they are different from worldly philosophies, and how they (gospel standards) will bring them peace, as the Savior promised in this scripture.

Review Resource Material #1-8 (pages 133-135), and Suggested Activity #1 (page 133) in Young Women Manual 3*.

1. Find and circle the gospel standards in the word find and highlight any that are of a special challenge to you.
2. Find the world philosophies word(s) found on the right that are opposite to the gospel standard on the left. EXAMPLE: "Astrology" (using the stars to pretend to tell fortunes) is opposite of our gospel standards of a "patriarchal blessing," where we receive direct revelation from our Heavenly Father as to our purpose and direction in this life. We also receive this direct revelation in our personal prayers, through the prophet, church leaders, and parents who are inspired to lead and guide us.
3. Unscramble the world philosophies (words) and write them in the blank column on the right.
ANSWERS (astrology, pornography, immorality, harmful substances, civil marriage, divorce, and abortion).
4. From the highlighted gospel standards (see #1 above), challenge yourself to study these gospel standards in the scriptures, *Era* and *Ensign* Church magazines and church books, learning the word of the Lord and his prophets until you feel secure and at peace with these standards.

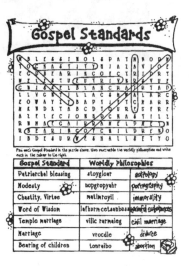

THOUGHT TREAT: Gospel Goodie Sack. Copy wordstrips (shown above/right). Cut out wordstrips and tape or glue to a variety of candies and place in a bag for young women to remember the sweetness the gospel brings. Gospel Goodie Sack wordstrips using Smartie candies, gummy worms, and Snicker bars:

Be a smarty and repent!
Don't be a worm, serve others.
Don't be a nerd, say a kind word.
Don't snicker at the truth.

COLOR SYMBOL: Color floral symbol on activity and scripture card. File activity in Young Women Value-able Journal behind the value tab.

Choice & Accountability (orange poppy)

PERSONAL PROGRESS* GOALS:
Beehive 2 (Choice & Accountability 2),
Mia Maid 1 (Choice & Accountability 2, 3),
Mia Maid 2 (Choice & Accountability 2, 3, 4, 6)

MIDWEEK ACTIVITY: *For the Strength of Youth Review.* Review this pamphlet published by the Church*. Ask young women to write their personal questions and put them in a box. Have the bishop or youth leader answer the questions during the next meeting.

Gospel Standards

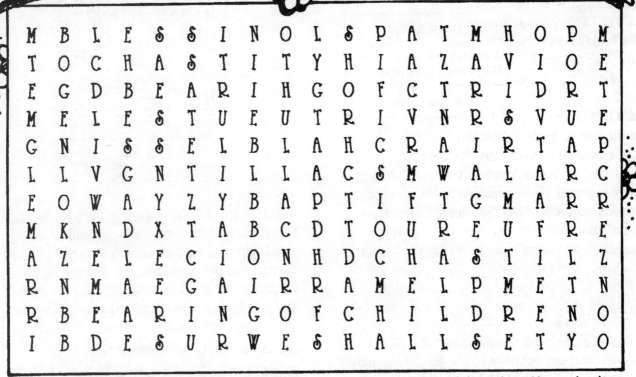

```
M B L E S S I N O L S P A T M H O P M
T O C H A S T I T Y H I A Z A V I O E
E G D B E A R I H G O F C T R I D R T
M E L E S T U E U T R I V N R S V U E
G N I S S E L B L A H C R A I R T A P
L L V G N T I L L A C S M W A L A R C
E O W A Y Z Y B A P T I F T G M A R R
M K N D X T A B C D T O U R E U F R E
A Z E L E C I O N H D C H A S T I L Z
R N M A E G A I R R A M E L P M E T N
R B E A R I N G O F C H I L D R E N O
I B D E S U R W E S H A L L S E T Y O
```

Find each Gospel Standard in the puzzle above, then unscramble the worldly philosophies and write each in the column to the right.

Gospel Standard	Worldly Philosophies	
Patriarchal blessing	stoygloar	
Modesty	nopgropyahr	
Chastity, Virtue	matimroyil	
Word of Wisdom	lafhurm cetsanbuss	
Temple marriage	vilic rarmaieg	
Marriage	vrocdie	
Bearing of children	tonraibo	

Lesson #38	**HEALTHY HABITS:** My Body Is a Temple
	(1 Corinthians 3:16 fitness plan tent card)

YOU'LL NEED: Copy of Bite-size memorize scripture and fitness plan (page 88) for each young woman, pencils, and colored markers.

Review Scripture discussion "You should" and "You should not" (page 138), Conclusion Scripture and testimony, and Lesson Application (page 140) in Young Women Manual 3*

ACTIVITY: (1) Read 1 Corinthians 3:16 on the tent card and talk about the meaning of this scripture. (2) Below "My Fitness Fun Plan of Healthy Habits," write habits you select that you want to improve. Write when you will do them in the "Morning, Noon, and Night" blocks.

COLOR SYMBOL: Color floral symbol on activity and scripture card. File activity in Young Women Value-able Journal behind the value tab.

Choice & Accountability (orange poppy)

PERSONAL PROGRESS* GOALS:
Beehive 1 (Knowledge 4), Beehive 2 (Knowledge 1, 5, 6, Choice & Accountability 6)

THOUGHT TREAT: Apple a Day. Give each young woman a small crisp apple to munch on as you talk about the reason they say, *"Eat an apple a day to keep the doctor away."* Here's why:
1. Apples satisfy your hunger in between meals.
2. Apples are full of vitamins and minerals.
3. Apples stabilize the blood sugar so you don't crave sweets.
4. Apples are known as *"nature's toothbrush,"* cleaning your teeth as you chew.
5. Apples help prevent gum disease as they massage the gums while you chew.
6. Apples are 80% water and high in fiber, helping cleanse the body of toxins. So, if you can, eating two a day is even better than *"one a day."*

MIDWEEK ACTIVITIES:
1. Couch Potato Motivators. As you write on the blackboard, ask young women help you list "couch potato" activities that are unhealthy and "perky potato" activities that are healthy.
IDEAS: Couch Potato: Watch television for hours at a time, overeating while watching television, eating junk food, not drinking enough water, not exercising. Perky Potato: Exercise, clean house vigorously, don't watch TV when you eat so you can think about and enjoy every bite. Snack on fruit and vegetables (preparing ahead to take with you when you are away from home).

2. Inner and Outer Beauty Workshop. Inner Beauty: Share ideas on grooming, e.g., skin and hair care, hair styling, simple natural-looking makeup ideas, nails, and clothing style and care. Remind young women that appearance is seen first, but it will not leave a lasting impression. Outer Beauty: The beauty that is found within that radiates through their countenance is the beauty that endures. If you spend as much time with the spiritual side as you do your appearance, you will radiate this inner beauty outwardly. To develop this inner beauty, read the scriptures, Church books and magazines, develop your talents, brighten someone's day, smile, and serve others. J.M. Barrie, author of *Peter Pan*, said, "Those who bring sunshine into the lives of others cannot keep it from themselves."

Know ye not
that ye are
the temple of
God, and that
the Spirit of God
dwelleth in you?

1 Corinthians 3:16

My Fitness Plan of Healthy Habits

Morning

Noon

Night

Lesson #39	**INDIVIDUAL WORTH:** I Am a Daughter of God
	(Great Worth and Value Grab Bag of valuable reminders)

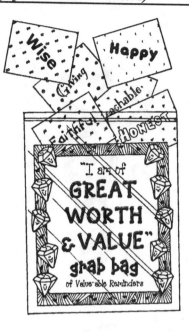

YOU'LL NEED: Copy of grab bag label and character trait cards (pages 90-91), and a zip-close plastic sandwich bag for each young woman, pencils, and colored markers.

ACTIVITY: (1) Read Ether 12:27, then talk about weaknesses and how we can become strong through reading the

> *Review Scripture discussion (page 144) i n Young Women Manual 3**

scriptures. (2) Share this Great Worth and Value Grab Bag full of character traits that will bring blessings. Remind young women of the journal cover message: *"I am of great worth and value, according to my Heavenly Father who knows me perfectly"* (or read D&C 18:10).

TO MAKE AND USE BAG: (1) Color and cut out grab bag label and character cards. Place label and cards inside a zip-close plastic sandwich bag. (2) Ask young women to take turns drawing a character card from bag. Read the card aloud, and tell what they can do to increase in that value. (3) Read Luke 2:52 and remind young women that Jesus increased in the mental, physical, spiritual, and social areas. Each day he improved. (4) Ask young women to take each card and write on the back ways they can strengthen their self-worth by acquiring each character trait. (5) Suggest to young women they carry one card in their purse or post it on their mirror to work on one each week. (6) See Thought Treat below (mint option).

COLOR SYMBOL: Color floral symbol on scripture card. File activity in Young Women Value-able Journal behind the value tab.

Individual Worth (red rose)

PERSONAL PROGRESS* GOALS:
Beehive 2 (Knowledge 7)

THOUGHT TREAT: Mints. (1) Place 15 Starlite mints in a plastic bag with the cards. The note on the bag reads, "Heavenly Father

'mint' for us to be happy!" (2) Ask young women to eat a mint each time they have tried to strengthen a character trait found on the cards.

MIDWEEK ACTIVITIES:
1. Individual Worth Testimonies. Ask young women to share how the gospel of Jesus Christ has given them feelings of individual worth.
2. Value-able Note. Write a note to each young woman expressing your love and admiration.
3. Self-talk. Talk about positive mental attitude and talking to ourselves in a positive way. Have a motivational speaker. Have young women gather and write their names at the top of a piece of paper. Pass the papers around, having each young woman and leader write a positive thing about the young woman. Ask the young women not to compare notes while they write. Then have each young woman look at her paper and add to her list the positive traits she believes she has. Then challenge them to do daily self-talk. Describe it and demonstrate. Examples: Say, "I am a daughter of God." Say this slowly and with feeling. Say, "I am a good listener," "I am gentle," "I am cute," "I am good dancer," etc. Encourage them to look at themselves in the mirror each day and say "I love you."

"I am of
**GREAT
WORTH
& VALUE**"
grab bag
of Value-able Reminders

Heavenly Father "mint"
for me to be happy!

"I am of
**GREAT
WORTH
& VALUE**"
grab bag
of Value-able Reminders

Heavenly Father "mint"
for me to be happy!

PATTERN: Individual Worth (Great Worth and Value Grab Bag valuable reminders)

Teachable	Humble	Giving
Loving	KiND	Truthful
Faithful	Dedicated	Wise
ReSPectful	Courteous	Friendly
HONEST	Trusting	Happy

Lesson #40	**LOVE:** I Will Love Myself and Others *(Matthew 22:36-39 service challenge tent card)*

YOU'LL NEED: Copy of tent card (page 93) for each young woman, pencils, and colored markers.

ACTIVITY:

Review Scripture discussion (page 145) in Young Women Manual 3*.

1. Challenge young women to memorize Matthew 22:36-39.
2. Brainstorm ways they can be of service to others. Suggest several of the Personal Progress goals (listed below).
3. Ask young women to write two ways they will love others and two ways they will love themselves.

"Master, which is the great commandment in the law?

Jesus said unto him, Thou shalt love the Lord thy God with all thy heart, and with all thy soul, and with all thy mind.

This is the first and great commandment.

And the second is like unto it, Thou shalt love thy neighbour as thyself."

Matthew 22:36-39

COLOR SYMBOL: Color floral symbol on activity and scripture card. File activity in Young Women Value-able Journal behind the value tab.

Individual Worth (red rose)

PERSONAL PROGRESS* GOALS:

Beehive 1 (Divine Nature 7, Individual Worth 7, 8),
Mia Maid 1 (Individual Worth 1, Good Works 4, 5)

THOUGHT TREAT: Heart Frosted Cupcakes. Tell young women that if their heart is full of love for others, they will in turn love themselves.

MIDWEEK ACTIVITIES:

1. Happiness Is a Gift You Give Yourself.

Tell young women, "As a young woman thinketh, so is she." You are what you think you are. Don't wait for someone to give you the positive feelings about yourself that you need. Have faith in yourself and know that you are a daughter of God. You are divine in nature and you can achieve your fullest potential if you pursue worthwhile goals, live the commandments, and pray for strength. This week practice smiling three times a day, thinking, "Happiness and confidence is a gift I must give myself."

2. Love Vitamins. Give young women a small bottle of candy pills (Smarties candies) with a note attached:

Give Yourself a Love Vitamin Daily
Each day *chew* a candy pill,
and *choose* something
positive to think and
say about you!

3. Pamper Yourself Night. Tell young women that the hardest commandment for some to obey is to love themselves. Get together, do pedicures, manicures, make-overs, hair trims and styles, etc. Have someone there to coordinate it (a professional). Talk about sleep, nutrition, and exercise. Encourage young women to "sharpen the saw" to always look their best. This gives them more freedom to attend to others.

*Young Women Manual 3, Personal Progress, Family Home Evening Resource, and *Hymns* are published by
The Church of Jesus Christ of Latter-day Saints, Salt Lake City, Utah.

92

2 Ways I Will Love Myself:

2 Ways I Will Love Others:

"Master, which is the great commandment in the law?

Jesus said unto him, Thou shalt love the Lord thy God with all thy heart, and with all thy soul, and with all thy mind.

This is the first and great commandment.

And the second is like unto it, Thou shalt love thy neighbour as thyself."

Matthew 22:36-39

Lesson #41	**DEPENDABILITY:** I Will Be Dependable
	(Decision Determines Destiny planner)

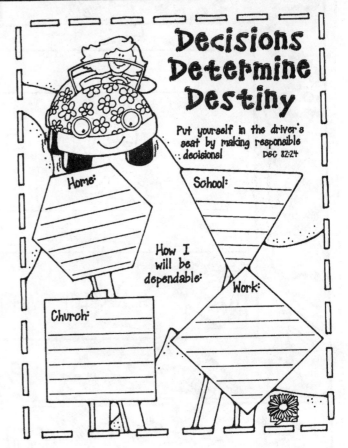

YOU'LL NEED: Copy of decision poster (page 95) for each young woman, pencils, and colored markers.

ACTIVITY: Tell young women that every decision they make can determine their destiny. They can put themselves in the driver's seat by making responsible decisions. They control their destiny.

Review Scripture (D&C 82:24) and Teacher discussion (page 149) in Young Women Manual 3*.

1. Read D&C 82:24. Tell young women that the celestial kingdom can be their destiny if they are steadfast in keeping the commandments.
2. Challenge young women to make responsible decisions each day at HOME, SCHOOL, CHURCH, and WORK as they think about being dependable. Make decisions by writing in ways you can be dependable.

COLOR SYMBOL: Color floral symbol on activity and scripture card. File activity in Young Women Value-able Journal behind the value tab.

Good Works (yellow sunflower)

PERSONAL PROGRESS* GOALS:
Beehive 1 (Choice & Accountability 5-7),
Beehive 2 (Knowledge 7, Integrity 2),
Mia Maid 1 (Knowledge 1, 9),
Mia Maid 2 (Knowledge 4-7, Integrity 2),
Laurel 1 & 2 Project 9 (page 79)

THOUGHT TREAT: Lifesaver Car. Glue four Lifesavers candies to a package of Lifesavers candies to create wheels. Tell young women they can drive safely each day by making dependable decisions and being steadfast in those decisions. Decisions determine destiny, allowing us to make it to the celestial kingdom (D&C 82:24).

MIDWEEK ACTIVITIES:
1. "Thanks, Mom, for Being Dependable" Breakfast. Help young women cook and serve breakfast to their moms. They can come in their pajamas. Have each young woman tell how her mom is dependable and what she admires about her. Take pictures of each young women with her mom. This can also be done with grandmothers and aunts.

2. Success in the Home. Quote President David O. McKay, who said, *"No success can compensate for failure in the home."* Talk about ways you can concentrate on home success. Ask young women how they project themselves in the home. IDEAS: Spend time with the children, focusing on their needs: spiritually, mentally, physically, and socially. Care for yourself to feel good about you. Plan for a home career, in case you need to work. Have young women reflect on the times their mother was and wasn't home when they arrived. Focus on the future now and begin to prepare, for tomorrow is just around the corner. Plan for an eternal marriage, as families can be together forever.

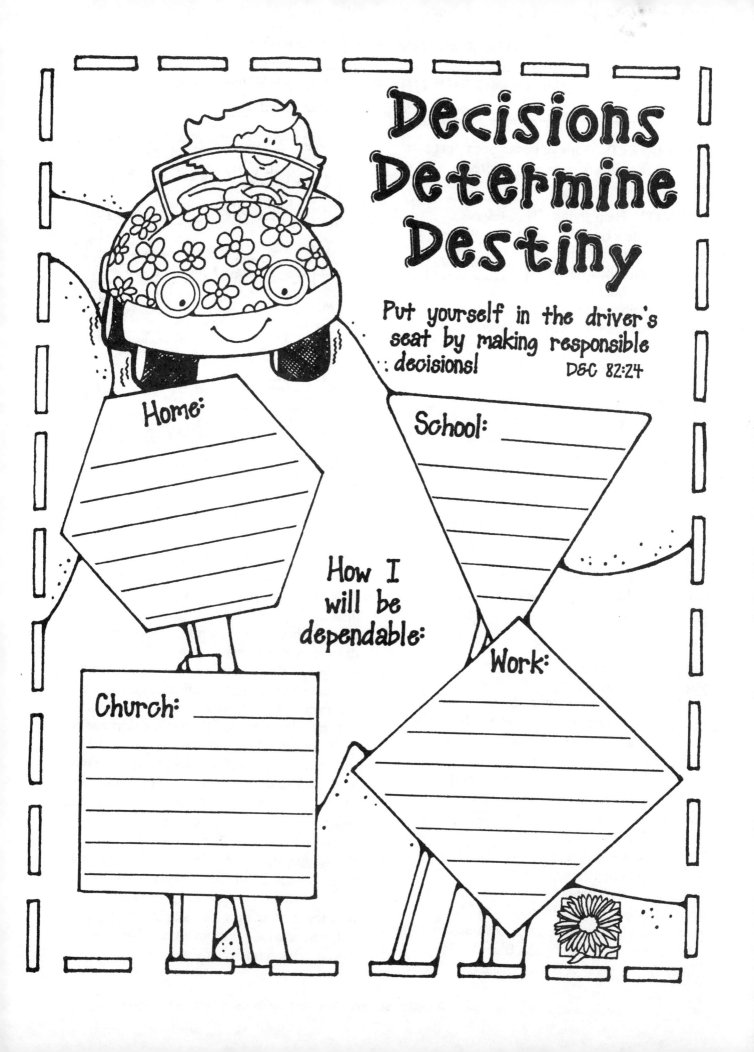

Decisions Determine Destiny

Put yourself in the driver's seat by making responsible decisions!   D&C 82:24

Home: _____

School: _____

How I will be dependable:

Church: _____

Work: _____

| Lesson #42 | **PREPARING FOR CHANGE:** I Will Stay Close to the Lord |
| | *(Changing Caterpillar - poster poem)* |

YOU'LL NEED: Copy of poster poem (page 97) for each young woman, and colored markers.

ACTIVITY: Help young women create a teaching tool they can take home and share with their family during family home evening. Color poster and learn poem. Ask young women to place poster on their wall to remind them to stay close to Spirit of the Holy Ghost, who will guide them in making changes.

> *Review Teacher presentation (page 154) in Young Women Manual 3*.*

COLOR SYMBOL: Color floral symbol on activity and scripture card. File activity in Young Women Value-able Journal behind the value tab.

Faith (white lily)

THOUGHT TREAT: <u>Gummy Caterpillars</u>. Purchase gummy worms and tell young women that even though caterpillars look like worms, deep down inside they have potential. They struggle and struggle and finally reach their potential.

MIDWEEK ACTIVITIES:

1. <u>Learn that "Practice Makes Progress</u>. Each time you do something that is difficult, it becomes easier the next time. So take the plunge!" Challenge young women to make a list of difficult tasks and set goals to achieve, e.g., starting with specific Personal Progress goals.

2. <u>"The Only Thing Consistent Is Change."</u> Change comes! The Lord knows what is coming. We do not need a crystal ball or psychic reading to be prepared for the future. The Holy Ghost will prompt us and guide us.

3. <u>Learn About Change</u>. Read stories about young men and women from the *Era* who made changes in their lives. Show MORMONAD posters (available at the Church Distribution Center), e.g., "Rise Above the Blues," "There's a Way Out," "Service: Get a Handle on it," etc.

4. <u>Develop Strong Habits</u>. Give each young woman a calendar and 21 stickers. Have then enter their goal for change at the top of the calendar and concentrate on that goal for 21 days. Place the stickers on the calendar the days they tried the new habit. It takes 21 days to change a habit. If you work consistently for 21 days straight, you have a new habit.

5. <u>Change Relay</u>. Have a relay race with a box of clothing in the center. Divide into two teams. Each young woman must run, put on an outfit over her clothing, which includes a skirt and top, a hat, gloves, a belt, and glasses, and model as she walks around a chair 4 feet away. She must walk back to the box and take off the apparel and return to her team. All young women could receive a diaper pin pinned on a note that reads: "Prepare for Change."

6. <u>Change Skit</u>. Have some bags of clothes and accessories and hand them to young women. Divide them into groups and give them 20 minutes to come up with a skit about change. Let them use their imaginations. Share the skits as you enjoy refreshments.

The NEW ME!

Change can be a
scary thing,
Like the caterpillar,
I must find my wings.
Heavenly Father created
me to move.
He knows that day by day
I will improve.
I must decide to make
the change soon,
To crawl inside my
spiritual cocoon.

While inside this place
called earthly home,
I pray and search.
I'm not alone.
Then one day, after
struggles and pain,
I win the prize of eternal reign.
A butterfly I've become.
I tell Heavenly Father
that his work I've done.

| Lesson #43 | **FRIENDSHIPS:** I Will Improve My Association With Others |
| | *(Moroni 7:45 Charity Chart challenge)* |

YOU'LL NEED: Copy of Charity Chart (page 99) for each young woman, and markers.

ACTIVITY: Help young women memorize Moroni 7:45 and think of five ways they can improve their relationship with at least one person. Write these five ways on the border of the Charity Chart.

Review Scripture discussion and Lesson Application (page 157) in Young Women Manual 3*.

COLOR SYMBOL: Color floral symbol on activity and scripture card. File activity in Young Women Value-able Journal behind the value tab.

Individual Worth (red rose)

PERSONAL PROGRESS* GOALS:
Beehive 2 (Good Works 1),
Mia Maid 1 (Divine Nature 3, Individual Worth 5, Choice & Accountability 1),
Mia Maid 2 (Integrity 4)

THOUGHT TREAT: Charity Charm Bracelet. Thread five different gummy type candies or Lifesavers on a licorice string for young women to tie around their wrists. As they eat the charm bracelet in class, ask them to share five ways they can be charitable to others.

MIDWEEK ACTIVITIES:

1. **Friendship.** Encourage young women to give their best ideas on how to acquire friends and be a friend. Tell them that these skills will help them in relationships with their family, friends, dates, and eventually a marriage friendship. A friend is someone with whom you have interests in common, you share basic values, and someone you have learned to accept and be around. IDEAS: ❤Look a person in the eye when you speak to them ❤Show gratitude ❤Confide in them ❤Apologize and admit when you are wrong ❤Be forgiving ❤Simply listen rather than give advice ❤Act interested ❤ Say thank you for compliments given you (it shows you value their thinking) ❤Help that friend feel important (someone said "It's nice to feel like

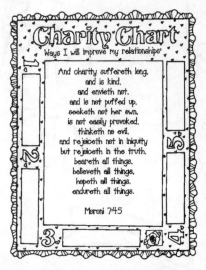

you're that person's only friend, even though you know you are not.")
❤ Don't look around at others when your friend is talking to you (pay attention), If others say "hello," or want to enter the conversation, include them without excluding the friend you are talking to ❤ remember names ❤ Be careful not to have so many friends that you stretch your energy too far (you need time for yourself and your family) ❤ Find a common subject of interest for which you can communicate ❤ Let others know you want their friendship instead of assuming they will discover it on their own.

2. **Friendships with Young Men.** Remind young women to treat young men as friends by paying attention to their thoughts, feelings, and accomplishments. Hopefully you will marry a young man who is your best friend. "Happy is the man that getteth understanding" (Proverbs 3:13). Communicate from the start. Share your likes and dislikes, and believe in his potential to serve a mission and to serve the Lord.

3. **"Pick"et a Friend.** Gather young women and make picket signs, e.g., "We love Rachel," etc. Go to young woman's home, and picket her home. Stick little signs on her lawn expressing love and friendship, e.g. "You are tops!," "We ❤ you," or "You're super!" Leave a plate of cookies on the porch; or better yet, get a jug of milk (placing a sign on it to invite her out to Young Women's). This also could be done with several young women or young men. If they are home, sit on the porch with cookies, and chat.

Charity Chart

Ways I will improve my relationships:

1

5

2

And charity suffereth long,
and is kind,
and envieth not,
and is not puffed up,
seeketh not her own,
is not easily provoked,
thinketh no evil,
and rejoiceth not in iniquity
but rejoiceth in the truth,
beareth all things,
believeth all things,
hopeth all things,
endureth all things.

Moroni 7:45

3

4

Lesson #44	**PLANNING:** **I Will Avoid Crisis Living** *(Time Tracker journal)*

YOU'LL NEED: Copy of Time Tracker journal (page 101) for each young woman, pencils, and colored markers.

ACTIVITY:

> *Review Teacher presentation and wordstrips (page 161) and Lesson Application (page 162) in Young Women Manual 3*.*

1. Encourage young women to manage their time and "not run faster or labor more than they have strength." Read Mosiah 4:27 and D&C 10:4, as found on the motivation poster "My Time Tracker."

2. Help young women write on their Time Tracker journal ways they can: "Establish Priorities," "Eliminate Unimportant Things," "Improve Work and Study Habits," and "Recognize Limitations."

3. Ask young women to try these four ways to help them track their time daily. Encourage them to use a calendar and track their time.

COLOR SYMBOL: Color floral symbol on activity and scripture card. File activity in Young Women Value-able Journal behind the value tab.

Choice & Accountability (orange poppy)

PERSONAL PROGRESS* GOALS:
Beehive 1 (Choice & Accountability 1)

THOUGHT TREAT: Clock Cookies. Frost and decorate sugar cookies with a smile face in the center and lines for hands on clock, creating these with frosting in a tube. Stick small candies on the 12, 3, 6, and 9 points of the clock. Tell young women that time will pass and goals will not be achieved, unless they plan their time. Encourage them to schedule their Personal Progress goals to complete each one on time.

MIDWEEK ACTIVITIES:

1. Plan Ahead. Gather young women together and say you are making cookies. Do not bring the eggs. Have the young women go to someone's house close to the church and borrow eggs. If possible pre-arrange with a few people to not have the needed eggs. They can then direct young women to another house, perhaps next door. When they find eggs, begin to make the cookies, then say, "Oh, I forgot the milk." Ask young women to get the milk from a pre-assigned home. As you sit and eat cookies, talk about planning ahead, making lists, getting things done in order, etc. This could be quite fun if "planned" well.

2. Plan to Succeed. Ask young women and leaders to share their ideas on planning for success. IDEAS: Have a place for everything and have everything in its place. Give away things you don't absolutely need. Plan your day in detail with a calendar or planner. Allow time for flexibility (don't plan your schedule too tightly). Take care of priorities first. Plan time for your family and for service. Make checklists and check them often. Plan a healthy diet, exercise, and drink plenty of water. Plan self-time, time to relax, time to read, and time to think. Pray and read the scriptures. Plan a weekly family home evening. Plan for a career (especially a home career). Plan and schedule their Personal Progress goals and activities.

3. Stress Reduction. Ask young women and leaders to share their ideas on ways to reduce stress. IDEAS: Focus on your strengths and how they can help you in stressful times. Develop a sense of humor. Cry. Laugh. Take a break—walk in the fresh air. Exercise. Listen to music you like. Talk to parents, family, and Heavenly Father about problems and really listen. Accept your school, home, church, and work responsibilities. Schedule priorities. Save for things you will need in the future. Plan your time. Change habits that cause stress. Eat healthfully, avoiding junk food.

*Young Women Manual 3 and Personal Progress books are published by The Church of Jesus Christ of Latter-day Saints, Salt Lake City, Utah.

Mosiah 4:27

And see that all things are done in wisdom and order. . . . . .

. . . be diligent, that thereby [you] might win the prize . .

TIME TRACKER

How will I make the best use of my time?

Establish priorities: _____
_____
_____

Eliminate unimportant things: _____
_____
_____

Improve work and study habits: _____
_____
_____

Recognize my limitations: _____
_____
_____

Lesson #45	**VOCATION: I Will Choose My Vocation Wisely** (I Give a Hoot! About My Vocation future focus planner)

YOU'LL NEED: Copy several future focus planner pages (page 103) for each young woman, pencils, and markers.

ACTIVITY:
Talk about the owl, who symbolizes being wise, patient, and introspective

Review Suggested Activities and Scripture discussion (page 165) in Young Women Manual 3*.

(can see in the dark). Read D&C 9:7-9 and say, "If we pray about our choices, we can see through obscurity [clouded darkness] as the wise owl is able to do."
1. Focus on your future by completing this planner form for each vocational choice.
2. Give young women several forms. Encourage them to pray about their future vocation.
3. Encourage young women to consider a home vocation, something they can do at home to earn money while they raise their children.

COLOR SYMBOL: Color floral symbol on activity and scripture card. File activity in Young Women Value-able Journal behind the value tab.

Choice & Accountability (orange poppy)

THOUGHT TREAT: Wise Owl Gummy Treats. Give each young women some candy gummy mice or worms. Say, "Like the wise owl hunting for food, we can hunt diligently for our education and develop our talents. This way we can provide for our families, if necessary."

MIDWEEK ACTIVITIES:
1. Noble Career. Pull scriptures and quotes from prophets and General Authorities that talk about careers and vocations and the role of women. Impress upon them a desire to first fulfill their responsibilities of wives and mothers, the most noble career. Assure them that knowledge and skills are really important. Guide them through choices that can give them great satisfaction and joy in both areas (work and family). Talk about reserving full-time careers for the right time and the importance of family first.

Talk about careers that can be done in the home. Speakers could give tours of their businesses in their homes.
2. **Steps to Choose Careers.** Encourage young women to take the time to choose one or more careers so they can begin planning for their future. IDEAS: ✆ Learn about career choices ✆ Learn about educational opportunities in your area ✆ Learn about scholarship ✆ Discuss subjects that will help with vocation and family life ✆ Learn good personal study habits ✆ Review school grades to determine how you can improve, then increase study time.
3. **Study Habits.** Share good study habits. IDEAS: ✆ Organize ✆ Schedule time ✆ Study the same place every day ✆ Study without television, distracting music, and friends ✆ Pray and ask for the Spirit to be with you ✆ Write vocabulary and spelling words and items to memorize on cards and post on the mirror.
✆ Take short breaks and get right back to study. Ralph Waldo Emerson said, "Concentration is the secret of strength."

I GIVE A HOOT!

about my vocation.

Vocation I'm interested in:

_____

Whooo I interviewed that has
this vocation: _____

_____

His / Her comments were: _____

_____

_____

_____

Place of employment visited: _____

_____

What I read about my vocation: _____

_____

_____

_____

My feelings about this vocation: _____

_____

_____

_____

Lesson #46	**MONEY MANAGEMENT:** I Will Manage My Money Wisely
	(Budget Brainstorm poster)

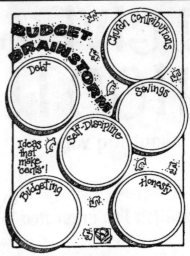

YOU'LL NEED: Copy of Budget Brainstorm poster (page 105) for each young woman, pencils, and colored markers.

ACTIVITY: Say to young women, "A penny for your thoughts," and hand them a penny to hold as you brainstorm

> Review Quotations and discussion #1-6 (pages 166-167), and Suggested Activity (page 168) in Young Women Manual 3*.

about budget ideas. Young women can take ideas home to post in their room or write in their journals to think about money management.

IDEAS THAT MAKE "CENTS" (SENSE):
1. <u>Church Contributions</u> (pay tithes and offerings first and blessings will come).
2. <u>Debt</u> (live within your income).
3. <u>Savings</u> (live within your earnings and put something away for a rainy day).
4. <u>Self-Discipline</u> (do without that which you cannot pay for).
5. <u>Budgeting</u> (plan money to avoid debt).
6. <u>Honesty</u> (always ask, is it right?).
OTHER "CENTS"-ABLE IDEAS: <u>Pending Spending</u>: Place money earned in a special envelope labeled "pending spending." This means that tithing needs to be paid before money is spent. <u>No "Mon" (money) No Fun</u>: Plan activities that don't require a lot of cash, and you can have fun without the worry of needing extra money.

COLOR SYMBOL: Color floral symbol on activity and scripture card. File activity in Young Women Value-able Journal behind the value tab.

Choice & Accountability (orange poppy)

PERSONAL PROGRESS* GOALS:
<u>Mia Maid 2 </u>(Knowledge 1)

THOUGHT TREAT: <u>Money Muffins</u>. Bake muffins and frost a dollar $ symbol on top. Tell young women that it's not how much money you make, but how you budget your money that counts.

MIDWEEK ACTIVITIES:
1. <u>**Pending Spending**</u>. Talk about ways you can put off spending to focus on priorities. Help young women picture themselves in the future starting a family on a budget. Help them visualize themselves in a budget-tight environment now, so that when they are in college and/or married, they can spend wisely. IDEAS: $ Place money earned in an envelope labeled "Pending Spending," until they can take out tithing and savings, and divide the balance of the money into envelopes to plan for upcoming events and purchases. $ Plan ahead where your money will be spent, e.g., gifts, greeting cards, vacation, or clothes. $ Plan ahead for birthdays, holidays, and special days to purchase gifts. $ Save for a mission and college. $ Place this money in a savings account and learn what interest can do.
2. <u>Food for All Planning Session</u>. Tell young women they will be eating a meal together. Give each young woman $2.00 and take them to the grocery store to choose and purchase the most food for their money. Young women can prepare and share the food they purchased. See what happens. Be prepared with can opener, napkins, and tableware. This is a good time to plan future activities that are inexpensive or that cost nothing. While eating, talk about the nutrition of each food and which items offered the most nutrition for the money.

*Young Women Manual 3 and Personal Progress books are published by The Church of Jesus Christ of Latter-day Saints, Salt Lake City, Utah.

Lesson #47 **PROPHETS: I Will Listen to the Latter-day Prophets**
(PROPHET PONDER journal)

YOU'LL NEED: Copy of journal (page 107) for each young woman, pencils, and markers.

ACTIVITY:
Talk to young women about taking notes when the prophet, his apostles, or other

Review Preparation #1 (page 170) in Young Women Manual 3*.

General Authorities talk. Start by writing on the PROPHET PONDER journal page, notes from the living prophet's talk in general conference (watch it on video or read it in the *Ensign*). Ask young women to review notes, placing a star (*) by ideas they want to share with someone. Then ask young women to share these important ideas in a Young Woman meeting.

COLOR SYMBOL: Color floral symbol on activity and scripture card. File activity in Young Women Value-able Journal behind the value tab.

Knowledge (green ivy)

THOUGHT TREAT: Prophet Punch. Give each young woman a drink of punch and say, "This is Prophet Punch. As we sip, let's review some of the things the prophets have told us to do to be temple worthy."

MIDWEEK ACTIVITIES:
1. Testimony Time Machine. Assign each young woman a prophet from the scriptures or the latter-day prophets. Ask them to dress like this prophet (to the best of their ability without expense) and give a 2 ½ minute talk on this prophet's testimony. Tell a story that the prophet told. Arrange these stories chronologically, writing the names of these prophets on the blackboard. Write Testimony Time Machine on the board. Then ask young woman give their prophet's testimony.
2. Conference Review Game using quotes from President Ezra Taft Benson. Tell young women that we can learn from all the prophets.

Photocopy the quotes (page 170-173 in the *Young Women Manual 3**), and cut up into wordstrips. Place them in a box labeled "A Latter-day Prophet Speaks." Ask young women to take turns drawing a message from the box, reading the message ahead of time, reading the message aloud, or saying it in her own words, then explain what it means to her.
3. Conference Talk Conversations. Divide the young women into groups of two or three. Assign each group a conference talk to review, from the *Ensign*. Ask each group to read the talk, outline the key points, and then make up a conversation they can share (like a skit) in front of the other young women.
4. Prophet Portraits. Assign a latter-day prophet to each young woman. Leaders may also do this activity. Have them research their prophet and come prepared to tell about him and what he was most famous for. Tell of experiences that are faith promoting. Have the pictures displayed and have speaker hold her prophet's picture as she gives her presentation.
5. "Windows of Heaven." Watch the movie (found in your ward library) and pop popcorn together. Have other refreshments that start with the letter "P" like pop, potato chips, or pretzels.

Young Women Manual 3 and *Personal Progress* books are published by The Church of Jesus Christ of Latter-day Saints, Salt Lake City, Utah.

PROPHET PONDER

Fill in the blanks as you read or listen to the prophet's message. Remember to always ponder and pray about his words.

Date:_____

Prophet: _____

His Message: _____

_____

_____

_____

_____

_____

_____

_____

_____

_____

_____

_____

_____

His testimony: _____

_____

_____

_____

_____

_____

Front cover

My Testimony Grows as I Study the Scriptures

Name:_____

Back cover

My Testimony Grows as I Study the Scriptures

Moroni's Words: The Book of Mormon Promise

Moroni 10:4-5 "And when ye shall receive these things, I would exhort you that ye would ask God, the Eternal Father, in the name of Christ, if these things are not true; and if ye shall ask with a sincere heart with real intent, having faith in Christ, he will manifest the truth of it unto you. And by the power of the Holy Ghost ye may know the truth of all things."

Inside front first page

My Testimony Grows as I Study the Scriptures

I love ♡ to read the scriptures because they help my testimony to blossom and grow. Blessings come from reading the scriptures and obeying the commandments. "Thou shalt be like a watered garden" (Isaiah 58:2-14). With the scriptures I can: "BLOOM WHERE I'M PLANTED." Each week in Young Women I will receive a scripture that represents the value taught in the lesson. Then I will:

1. Find the scripture and fill in the missing words.
2. Color the value symbol the value color written at the bottom of the card. Example: Color the sunflower (shown right) "yellow," representing the value "Good Works."
3. Post scripture cards on my mirror during the week to ponder.
4. OPTION #1: Create a book by punching the two hearts (shown left) and tie a ribbon through holes in a bow. OPTION #2: Cut the heart border off and create a card file with A-Z dividers (to file cards by subject), or Young Women value divider tabs.

| My Testimony Grows as I Study the Scriptures |

HEAVENLY FATHER: I am a Daughter of God

Romans 8:16-17 "The Spirit itself beareth witness with our _ _ _ _ _ _ _, that we are the children of God: And if children, then _ _ _ _ _ _; heirs of God, and joint-heirs with Christ; if so be that we _ _ _ _ _ _ _ with him, that we may be also glorified together."

Young Women Value: Divine Nature (blue morning glory) Lesson #1 Manual 3

| My Testimony Grows as I Study the Scriptures |

JESUS CHRIST: I Will Strive to Make Jesus My Friend

D&C 88:62-63 "I say unto you, my friends, I leave these sayings with you to _ _ _ _ _ _ _ in your hearts, with this commandment which I give unto you, that ye shall _ _ _ _ _ upon me while I am near—Draw _ _ _ _ _ unto me and I will draw near unto you; _ _ _ _ _ me diligently and ye shall find me; ask, and ye shall receive; knock, and it shall be opened unto you."

Young Women Value: Faith (white lily) Lesson #2 Manual 3

| My Testimony Grows as I Study the Scriptures |

RIGHTEOUSNESS: I Will Draw Close to the Savior

D&C 19:23 "Learn of me, and _ _ _ _ _ _ _ to my words; walk in the _ _ _ _ _ _ _ _ _ of my Spirit, and you shall have _ _ _ _ _ _ in me."

Young Women Value: Divine Nature (blue morning glory) Lesson #3 Manual 3

My Testimony Grows as I Study the Scriptures

TEMPLE MARRIAGE: I Will Prepare to Be an Eternal Companion

Moses 3:18, 22 "I, the Lord God, said unto mine Only Begotten, that it was not good that __ __ __ should be __ __ __ __ __; wherefore, I will make an __ __ __ __ meet for him.... And the rib which I, the Lord God, had taken from man, made I a woman, and brought her unto the __ __ __."

Young Women Value: Divine Nature (blue morning glory) Lesson #4 Manual 3

My Testimony Grows as I Study the Scriptures

HOMEMAKING: I Will Create a Spiritual Environment in My Home

D&C 88:119 "Organize yourselves; prepare every needful thing; and establish a house, even a house of __ __ __ __ __ __ __, a house of __ __ __ __ __ __ __, a house of __ __ __ __ __ __, a house of __ __ __ __ __ __ __ __, a house of glory, a house of order, a house of God."

Young Women Value: Good Works (yellow sunflower) Lesson #5 Manual 3

My Testimony Grows as I Study the Scriptures

TEACHING: I Will Follow the Example of Jesus

D&C 88:77, 118 "I give unto you a commandment that ye shall __ __ __ __ __ __ one another the doctrine of the kingdom.... And as all have not faith, seek ye diligently and teach one another words of wisdom; yea, seek ye out of the __ __ __ __ books words of wisdom; seek learning, even by __ __ __ __ __ and also by __ __ __ __ __ __."

Young Women Value: Divine Nature (blue morning glory) Lesson #6 Manual 3

110

My Testimony Grows as I Study the Scriptures

PURPOSE IN LIFE: I Will Tune into the Lord's Will

Proverbs 3:5-6 "Trust in the
_ _ _ _ with all thine heart;
and lean not unto thine own
understanding. In all thy ways
acknowledge him, and he shall
_ _ _ _ _ _ thy paths."

Young Women Value: Divine Nature (blue morning glory) Lesson #7 Manual 3

My Testimony Grows as I Study the Scriptures

FAMILIES (Eternal): I Will Be Worthy of Eternal Blessings

D&C 131:1-4 "In the celestial glory there are three
heavens or degrees; And in order to obtain the
_ _ _ _ _ _ _ _, a man must enter into this
order of the priesthood [meaning the new and
everlasting covenant of _ _ _ _ _ _ _ _];
And if he does not, he cannot _ _ _ _ _ _ it.
He may enter into the other, but that is the end of
his kingdom; he cannot have an increase."

Young Women Value: Choice & Accountability (orange poppy) Lesson #8 Manual 3

My Testimony Grows as I Study the Scriptures

FAMILY UNITY: I Will Create Family Ties

4 Nephi 1:15-16 "And it came to pass that there
was no contention in the land, because of the
_ _ _ _ of God which did dwell in the
_ _ _ _ _ _ of the people. And there were no
envyings, nor strifes, nor tumults, nor whoredoms,
nor lyings, nor murders, nor any manner of
lasciviousness; and surely there could not be a
_ _ _ _ _ _ _ people among all the people who had been
created by the hand of God."

Young Women Value: Individual Worth (red rose) Lesson #9 Manual 3

| My Testimony Grows as I Study the Scriptures |

FAMILY ACTIVITIES: I Will Encourage Enjoyable Family Activities

Family Activities Can Be Simple or Complex
Alma 37:6 "I say unto you, that by
_ _ _ _ _ _ and simple things are great
things brought to pass; and small means in
many instances doth confound the
_ _ _ _ _." Family Home Evening doesn't need
to be elaborate, but it needs to be consistent week after week.

Young Women Value: Good Works (yellow sunflower) Lesson #10 Manual 3

| My Testimony Grows as I Study the Scriptures |

FAMILIES (Extended): I Will Be a Friend to Extended Family

John 13:34-35 "A new commandment
I give unto you, That ye _ _ _ _ _ one
another; as I have loved you, that ye also love
one another. By this shall all men know that
ye are my _ _ _ _ _ _ _ _ _ _ _, if ye
have love one to another."

Young Women Value: Good Works (yellow sunflower) Lesson #11 Manual 3

| My Testimony Grows as I Study the Scriptures |

PRIESTHOOD BLESSINGS From Heavenly Father

D&C 121:45-46 "Let thy bowels also be full of
charity towards all men, and to the household
of _ _ _ _ _, and let virtue garnish thy
_ _ _ _ _ _ _ _ unceasingly; then shall
thy confidence wax strong in the presence of
God; and the doctrine of the priesthood shall
distil upon thy _ _ _ _ as the dews from heaven."

Young Women Value: Individual Worth (red rose) Lesson #12 Manual 3

My Testimony Grows as I Study the Scriptures

PRIESTHOOD Blesses Families

D&C 121:36 "The rights of the priesthood are inseparably connected with the powers of _ _ _ _ _ _ _, and that the powers of heaven cannot be controlled nor handled only upon the principles of _ _ _ _ _ _ _ _ _ _ _ _ _ _ _ _ _ _ _."

Young Women Value: Individual Worth (red rose) Lesson #13 Manual 3

My Testimony Grows as I Study the Scriptures

RESTORATION: Jesus Christ's Church Is Restored

D&C 27:5-6 "The hour cometh that I will drink of the fruit of the vine with you on the earth, and with Moroni, whom I have sent unto you to reveal the Book of Mormon, containing the _ _ _ _ _ _ _ _ of my everlasting gospel ... And also Elias, to whom I have committed the keys of bringing to pass the restoration of all things spoken by the mouth of all the holy prophets since the world began, concerning the last days."

Young Women Value: Good Works (yellow sunflower) Lesson #14 Manual 3

My Testimony Grows as I Study the Scriptures

ETERNAL LIFE: Blessings of the House of Israel

Moses 1:39 "For behold, this is my work and my _ _ _ _ _ _ —to bring to pass the immortality and eternal life of _ _ _."

2 Nephi 9:39 "Remember, to be carnally-minded is death, and to be spiritually-minded is _ _ _ _ _ eternal."

Young Women Value: Divine Nature (blue morning glory) Lesson #15 Manual 3

My Testimony Grows as I Study the Scriptures

TEMPLE ENDOWMENT: I Will Prepare for Eternal Life

D&C 124:40-41 "Let this house be built unto my name, that I may _ _ _ _ _ _ _ mine ordinances therein unto my people; For I deign to reveal unto my church things which have been _ _ _ _ _ hid from before the foundation of the world, things that pertain to the dispensation of the fulness of _ _ _ _ _ _."

Young Women Value: Choice & Accountability (orange poppy) Lesson #16 Manual 3

My Testimony Grows as I Study the Scriptures

TEMPLE PREPARATION:
I Will Prepare to Enter the Temple

D&C 97:15-17 "Inasmuch as my people build a house unto _ _ _ in the name of the Lord, and do not suffer any _ _ _ _ _ _ _ _ _ thing to come into it, that it be not defiled, my glory shall rest upon it; Yea, and my presence shall be there, for I will come into it, and all the _ _ _ _ _ in heart that shall come into it shall see God. But if it be defiled I will not come into it, and my glory shall not be there; for I will not come into _ _ _ _ _ _ _ temples."

Young Women Value: Divine Nature (blue morning glory) Lesson #17 Manual 3

My Testimony Grows as I Study the Scriptures

TEMPLE MARRIAGE: My Family Can Be Together Forever

D&C 132:19-20 "If a man marry a wife by my word, which is my _ _ _ _, and by the new and everlasting covenant, and it is sealed unto them by the Holy Spirit of promise, by him who is anointed, unto whom I have appointed this power and the _ _ _ _ _ of this priesthood; ... ye shall come forth in the first resurrection ... and shall inherit thrones, kingdoms, principalities, and _ _ _ _ _ _ _, dominions, ... Then shall they be gods, because they have no end."

Young Women Value: Divine Nature (blue morning glory) Lesson #18 Manual 3

My Testimony Grows as I Study the Scriptures

HERITAGE: I Will Pass on Righteous Traditions

Mosiah 1:5 "Were it not for these things, which have been __ __ __ __ and preserved by the hand of God, that we might __ __ __ __ and understand of his mysteries and have his commandments all ways before our eyes, that even our fathers would have dwindled in __ __ __ __ __ __ __ __ __."

Young Women Value: Individual Worth (red rose) Lesson #19 Manual 3

My Testimony Grows as I Study the Scriptures

MISSIONARY WORK: I Will Support Missionary Work

D&C 18:14-16 "Wherefore, you are called to cry repentance unto this people. And if it so be that you should __ __ __ __ __ all your days in crying repentance unto this people, and bring save it be __ __ __ soul unto me, how great shall be your __ __ __ with him in the kingdom of my Father. And now, if your joy will be great with one soul that you have brought unto me into the kingdom of my Father, how great will be your joy if you should bring many __ __ __ __ __ unto me!"

Young Women Value: Good Works (yellow sunflower) Lesson #20 Manual 3

My Testimony Grows as I Study the Scriptures

MISSIONARY SERVICE: Follow Prophets and Share the Gospel

3 Nephi 18:24 "Hold up your __ __ __ __ __ that it may shine into the world. Behold I am the light which ye shall hold up—that which ye have seen me do."
D&C 123:12, 16 "For there are many yet on the earth among all sects, parties, and denominations, who are __ __ __ __ __ __ __ __ by the subtle craftiness of men, whereby they lie in wait to deceive, and who are only kept from the truth because they know not where to __ __ __ __ it.... A very large ship is benefited very much by a very small helm in the time of a storm, by being kept workways with the wind and the waves."

Young Women Value: Good Works (yellow sunflower) Lesson #21 Manual 3

♡ ♡

My Testimony Grows as I Study the Scriptures

ETERNAL PERSPECTIVE: I Can Face Trials

D&C 93:24 "Truth is knowledge of things as they
_ _ _, and as they _ _ _ _, and as they
are to come."

Isaiah 55:8-9 "For my _ _ _ _ _ _ _ _ _ _
are not your thoughts, neither are my ways your
ways, saith the Lord. For as the heavens are higher than the
_ _ _ _ _ _, so are my ways higher than your ways, and my
thoughts than your thoughts."

Young Women Value: Knowledge (green ivy) Lesson #22 Manual 3

♡ ♡

My Testimony Grows as I Study the Scriptures

OPPOSITION Can Make Me Strong

D&C 121:7-8 "My son, peace be unto thy soul; thine
_ _ _ _ _ _ _ _ _ _ _ and thine
afflictions shall be but a small moment.
And then, if thou _ _ _ _ _ _ _ it well,
God shall exalt thee on high; thou shalt
triumph over all thy foes."

Young Women Value: Integrity (purple pansy) Lesson #23 Manual 3

♡ ♡

My Testimony Grows as I Study the Scriptures

AGENCY: I Will Follow Jesus Christ

2 Nephi 2:27-28 "Men are _ _ _ _ _ ... to choose
liberty and _ _ _ _ _ _ _ _ _ life, through the great
Mediator of all men, or to choose captivity and death,
according to the captivity and power of the devil; for he
seeketh that all men might be miserable like unto himself.
And now ... I would that ye should look to the great Mediator, and
hearken unto his great commandments; and be faithful unto his words,
and choose eternal life according to the will of his Holy Spirit."

Young Women Value: Choice & Accountability (orange poppy) Lesson #24 Manual 3

My Testimony Grows as I Study the Scriptures

OBEDIENCE: I Can Be Obedient

D&C 59:23 "He who doeth the
_ _ _ _ _ of righteousness
shall receive his _ _ _ _ _ _,
even peace in this world, and
eternal life in the world to come."

Young Women Value: Good Works (yellow sunflower) Lesson #25 Manual 3

My Testimony Grows as I Study the Scriptures

REPENTANCE: I Will Change My Thoughts and Behavior

Alma 41:10 "Do not suppose, because it
has been spoken concerning restoration,
that ye shall be restored from _ _ _
to happiness. Behold, I say unto you,
_ _ _ _ _ _ _ _ _ _ _ never was
happiness."

Young Women Value: Choice & Accountability (orange poppy) Lesson #26 Manual 3

My Testimony Grows as I Study the Scriptures

FORGIVENESS: I Will Forgive Myself and Others

D&C 58:42-43 "He who has repented of his _ _ _ _,
the same is forgiven, and I the Lord, remember them _ _
more." Mosiah 4:2-3 "They had viewed themselves in
their own carnal state, even less than the dust of the
earth. And they all cried aloud with one voice, saying: O have _ _ _
_ _, and apply the atoning blood of Christ that we may receive
forgiveness of our sins, and our hearts may be purified; for we believe in
Jesus Christ, the Son of God.... After they had spoken ... the Spirit of
the Lord came upon them, and they were filled with joy, having received
a remission of their _ _ _ _, and having peace of conscience ..."

Young Women Value: Individual Worth (red rose) Lesson #27 Manual 3

117

My Testimony Grows as I Study the Scriptures

CONSECRATION & SACRIFICE: I Will Sacrifice My
Time, Talents, and Means to Build up the Kingdom of God

D&C 88:22 "He who is not able to abide the
__ __ __ of a celestial kingdom
cannot abide a celestial glory."
Mosiah 2:34 "Ye are eternally
indebted to your heavenly Father,
to render to him __ __ __ that you
have and are."

Young Women Value: *Good Works (yellow sunflower) Lesson #28 Manual 3*

My Testimony Grows as I Study the Scriptures

CHANGE OF HEART: Faithful in Keeping the Commandments
Mosiah 4:6-7 "If ye have come to a knowledge of the
goodness of God, and his matchless power, and his
wisdom, and his patience, and his long-suffering
towards the children of men; and also, the atonement
..., that thereby salvation might come to him that
should put his trust in the Lord, and should be diligent in keeping
his commandments, and continue in the __ __ __ __ __ even unto
the __ __ __ of his life ... this is the man who receiveth salvation."

Young Women Value: *Choice & Accountability (orange poppy) Lesson #29 Manual 3*

My Testimony Grows as I Study the Scriptures

SCRIPTURE STUDY: I Love to Read the Scriptures
2 Timothy 3:15-16 "From a child thou hast known the
__ __ __ __ scriptures, which are able to make thee
wise unto salvation through faith which is in Christ
Jesus. All scripture is given by inspiration of God, and
is profitable for doctrine, for reproof, for correction, for
instruction in righteousness: That the man of God may
be __ __ __ __ __ __ __, throughly furnished unto all good works."
D&C 33:16 "The Book of Mormon and the __ __ __ __
scriptures are given of me for your instruction."

Young Women Value: Knowledge (green ivy) Lesson #30 Manual 3

My Testimony Grows as I Study the Scriptures

SERVICE IN THE CHURCH: I Will Serve the Lord

Joshua 24:15 "Choose you this day whom ye will serve; ... as for me and my __ __ __ __ __, we will serve the Lord."

Matthew 25:40 "Inasmuch as ye have done it unto one of the least of these my brethren, ye have done it unto __ __."

Young Women Value: Good Works (yellow sunflower) Lesson #31 Manual 3

My Testimony Grows as I Study the Scriptures

SERVICE IN THE COMMUNITY:
I Will Take Time to Serve

Moroni 7:13 "That which is of God inviteth and enticeth to do __ __ __ __ continually; wherefore, every thing which inviteth and enticeth to do good, and to __ __ __ __ God, and to __ __ __ __ __ him, is inspired of God."

Young Women Value: Good Works (yellow sunflower) Lesson #32 Manual 3

My Testimony Grows as I Study the Scriptures

FRIENDSHIP: Each Person is Divine and Eternal

D&C 18:10-11 "Remember the worth of souls is great in the __ __ __ __ __ of God. For, behold, the Lord your Redeemer suffered death in the flesh; wherefore he suffered the pain of __ __ __ men, that all men might repent and come unto him."

Young Women Value: Individual Worth (red rose) Lesson #33 Manual 3

119

| My Testimony Grows as I Study the Scriptures |

HONESTY: I Will Avoid Dishonesty and Its Consequences
D&C 42:20-21, 28-29 "Thou shalt not
__ __ __ __ __; and he that stealeth and will not
repent shall be cast out. Thou shalt not __ __ __;
he that lieth and will not repent shall be cast out.
Thou knowest my laws concerning these things are
given in my scriptures; he that sinneth and repenteth not shall be
cast __ __ __. If thou lovest me thou shalt __ __ __ __ __ me
and keep my commandments."

Young Women Value: Integrity (purple pansy) Lesson #34 Manual 3

| My Testimony Grows as I Study the Scriptures |

DATING DECISIONS: Dating Decisions Affect My Eternal Life

2 Nephi 9:39 "Remember the awfulness
in transgressing against the Holy God,
and also the awfulness of yielding to the
enticings of that cunning one.
Remember, to be carnally-minded is
death, and to be spiritually-minded is life
__ __ __ __ __ __ __."

Young Women Value: Choice & Accountability (orange poppy) Lesson #35 Manual 3

| My Testimony Grows as I Study the Scriptures |

MARRIAGE STANDARDS: I Will Acquire Positive Traits
to Attract a Positive Mate

D&C 25:14-15 "Continue in the spirit of
meekness, and beware of pride. Let thy soul
delight in thy husband, and the glory which
shall come upon him. Keep my commandments
continually, and a __ __ __ __ __ of
righteousness thou shalt receive. And except
thou do this, where I am you cannot come."

Young Women Value: Individual Worth (red rose) Lesson #36 Manual 3

| My Testimony Grows as I Study the Scriptures |

STANDARDS: I Can Cope With Worldliness as I
Live the Gospel Standards

Proverbs 3:5-6 "Trust in the Lord
with all thine __ __ __ __ __; and
lean not unto thine own
understanding. In all thy ways
acknowledge him, and he shall direct
thy __ __ __ __ __."

Young Women Value: Choice & Accountability (orange poppy) Lesson #37 Manual 3

| My Testimony Grows as I Study the Scriptures |

HEALTHFUL HABITS: My Body is a Temple

D&C 88:124 "Cease to be __ __ __ __; cease to
be unclean; cease to find fault one with another;
cease to sleep longer than is needful;
__ __ __ __ __ __ to thy bed early, that ye may
not be weary; __ __ __ __ __ early, that your
bodies and your minds may be invigorated."
D&C 89 (Word of Wisdom)

Young Women Value: Choice & Accountability (orange poppy) Lesson #38 Manual 3

| My Testimony Grows as I Study the Scriptures |

INDIVIDUAL WORTH: I Am a Daughter of God
D&C 18:10 "Remember the __ __ __ __ __ of souls
is great in the sight of God."
Ether 12:27: "If men come unto me I will show unto
them their weaknesses. I give unto men weakness
that they may be humble; and my grace is sufficient
for all men that humble themselves before me; for if they
__ __ __ __ __ __ themselves before me, and have faith in me, then
will I make weak things become __ __ __ __ __ __ unto them.."

Young Women Value: Individual Worth (red rose) Lesson #39 Manual 3

My Testimony Grows as I Study the Scriptures

LOVE: I Will Love Myself and Others

D&C 38:24 "Let every man esteem his brother as himself, and practise virtue and _ _ _ _ _ _ _ _ before me."

Young Women Value: Choice & Accountability (orange poppy) Lesson #40 Manual 3

My Testimony Grows as I Study the Scriptures

DEPENDABILITY: I Will Be Dependable

D&C 82:24 "For even yet the _ _ _ _ _ _ _ _ is yours, and shall be forever, if you fall _ _ _ from your steadfastness."

1 Nephi 3:7 "I will _ _ and _ _ the things which the Lord hath commanded, for I know that the Lord giveth _ _ commandments unto the children of men, save he shall prepare a way for them that they may accomplish the thing which he commandeth them."

Young Women Value: Good Works (yellow sunflower) Lesson #41 Manual 3

My Testimony Grows as I Study the Scriptures

PREPARING FOR CHANGE:
I Will Stay Close to the Lord

John 14:27 "_ _ _ _ _ I leave with you, my peace I give unto you: not as the world giveth, give I unto you. Let not your _ _ _ _ _ be troubled, neither let it be afraid."

Young Women Value: Faith (white lily) Lesson #42 Manual 3

My Testimony Grows as I Study the Scriptures

FRIENDSHIPS: I Will Improve My Association With Others

D&C 88:124 "Cease to find
_ _ _ _ _ one with another."

Ephesians 4:32 "Be ye _ _ _ _ one to
another, tenderhearted, forgiving one
another, even as God for Christ's sake hath
forgiven _ _ _."

Young Women Value: Individual Worth (red rose) Lesson #43 Manual 3

My Testimony Grows as I Study the Scriptures

PLANNING: I Will Avoid Crisis Living

D&C 10:4 "Do not _ _ _ faster or
_ _ _ _ _ more than you have strength and
means provided ... be diligent unto the end."
Mosiah 4:27 "See that all things are done in
wisdom and _ _ _ _ _; for it is not requisite
that a man should run faster than he has
strength... Be diligent, that thereby [ye] might win the
_ _ _ _ _; therefore, all things must be _ _ _ _
in order."

Young Women Value: Choice & Accountability (orange poppy) Lesson #44 Manual 3

My Testimony Grows as I Study the Scriptures

VOCATION: I Will Choose My Vocation Wisely

D&C 9:7-9 "You took no thought save it was
to ask me. But, behold, I say unto you, that
you must _ _ _ _ _ it out in your mind;
then you must _ _ _ me if it be right, and
if it is right I will cause that your bosom
shall _ _ _ _ within you; therefore, you shall
feel that it is right."

Young Women Value: Choice & Accountability (orange poppy) Lesson #45 Manual 3

My Testimony Grows as I Study the Scriptures

MONEY MANAGEMENT: I Will Manage My Money Wisely
Our financial management can affect us spiritually:
church contributions, debt, savings, self-discipline, budgeting, and honesty.

D&C 29:34 "All things unto me are
_ _ _ _ _ _ _ _ _ _, and not at any time
have I given unto you a law which was temporal;
neither any man, nor the children of men; neither
Adam, your father, whom I created."

Young Women Value: Choice & Accountability (orange poppy) Lesson #46 Manual 3

My Testimony Grows as I Study the Scriptures

PROPHETS: I Will Listen to the Latter-day Prophets

1 Nephi 22:31 "Wherefore, ye need not
suppose that I and my father are the only
ones that have _ _ _ _ _ _ _ _ _ _ _,
and also taught them. Wherefore, if ye shall
be obedient to the commandments and
_ _ _ _ _ _ _ to the end, ye shall be
saved at the last day."

Young Women Value: Knowledge (green ivy) Lesson #47 Manual 3

My Testimony Grows as I Study the Scriptures

MY FAVORITE SCRIPTURES:

_____
_____
_____
_____
_____
_____